# PRIVATE PLEASURE,
# PUBLIC PLIGHT

# PRIVATE PLEASURE, PUBLIC PLIGHT

## American Metropolitan Community Life in Comparative Perspective

### DAVID POPENOE

Transaction Books
New Brunswick (U.S.A.) and Oxford (U.K.)

Library of Congress Catalog Number: 84-16411
ISBN: 0-88738-030-1 (cloth)
Printed in the United States of America

**Library of Congress Cataloging in Publication Data**

Popenoe, David, 1932-
  Private pleasure, public plight.

  Includes index.
  1. Metropolitan areas—United States.   2. Sociology, Urban—United
States. 3. Community life. 4. Social problems. I. Title.

HT334. U5P66   1984        307.7′64′0973              84-16411
ISBN 0-88738-030-1

# Contents

# Preface

From a European viewpoint, the metropolitan areas of the United States appear shoddy and unmanaged. Looking beyond appearances into the social fabric of metropolitan life, the scene often is no more pleasant to behold. Urban and metropolitan areas in the United States have such social problems as juvenile deliquency, violent crime, and family breakdown in a magnitude far exceeding those of comparable areas in Europe. In comparative perspective, American metropolitan life has a marked vitality but also an undeniable pathos. How to account for the characteristics of U.S. metropolitan life, and their significance for contemporary American society and culture, are the main issues explored in this book.

The idea of writing this book evolved gradually during the 1970s as I annually shuttled between the United States and Europe on various research and teaching ventures. There is nothing better than such constant cross-cultural comparisons to bring into bold relief the conditions of one's own country and, given the diversity of European society, to check and check again tentative hypotheses that leap to mind. The research materials and observations in this book were developed over an eight-year period, starting in 1972 when I traveled with my family to Sweden for a year as a Fulbright scholar and visiting professor at the University of Stockholm. The many additional trips made later in the decade both to Sweden and to many other European countries included a six-month stay in England in 1978 at London's Centre for Environmental Studies.

But the true genesis of the book may well go back at least to the time I first became interested in urban and community studies, as an undergraduate, through reading Lewis Mumford's *The Culture of Cities*. Having grown up in a Los Angeles suburb, my appetite for comparative community studies became whetted, long before my first serious contact with European metropolitan life, through living in a small Ohio town, the central cities of Philadelphia and New York, and finally for the last several decades in Princeton, New Jersey. The major influences on the development of ideas presented herein are much too numerous to detail, but they most assuredly include my teachers at the University of Pennsylvania, my sociological colleagues at Rutgers University and the University of Stockholm, and my wife and family.

I would like publicly to acknowledge and thank (while at the same time absolving them of responsibility for any of my failings) the following colleagues who critically reviewed this manuscript: Robert Gutman, Lyn Lofland, and Jeffrey Slovak in the United States; Anthony D. King in the United Kingdom; and Åke Daun in Sweden.

In a study as wide-ranging as this it is impossible to list all of the sources that bear on particular themes. I have therefore been selective, noting mainly those principal sources that have influenced significantly my own thinking and that at the same time may be of interest to the general reader.

This book grows out of an earlier one, *The Suburban Environment: Sweden and the United States (1977).* That work was a comparative study in the sociology of housing, dealing with the social impact of variations in housing and the built environment. The present study is much broader in scope, looking at metropolitan life in general, and dealing with a wide range of social issues. In addition, it brings in another advanced society, England, to further expand the comparative focus.

# Introduction

*Ill fares the land, to hastening ills a prey,*
*Where wealth accumulates, and men decay.*
—Oliver Goldsmith, *The Deserted Village*

Could Goldsmith's words, written two hundred years ago at the dawn of the industrial revolution, be prophetic of our own age? The societies of the West, having reaped full economic benefit from the industrial and urban developments of the last two centuries, may be at the dawn of another new era. Called by some postindustrial, postcapitalist, and even postmodern, the new era is designated by the office instead of the factory, the computer supplanting the machine, and the metropolitan area in place of the town and the city.

As in Goldsmith's time, many things today seem amiss. Especially in the metropolitan areas, where 75 percent of our population live, the United States is the crucible of problems that belie our affluence, our freedom, and our democracy. Social problems range from loneliness, anxiety, and divorce, through alcoholism, drug abuse, and delinquency, to violent crime. Lewis Mumford once portrayed the situation of metropolitan dwellers with words that must at times strike a chord in each of us: "Increasingly they find themselves 'strangers and afraid,' in a world they never made: a world ever less responsive to direct human command, ever more empty of human meaning."[1]

If the published statistics are accurate, these social problems are getting worse, not better. In the incidence of some of the problems, notably divorce, drug abuse, delinquency, and violent crime, the United States ranks at the top of all nations, both those developed and those still developing. In alcoholism, we rank near the top. And although statistical measures are not available for loneliness and anxiety, few would deny that these problems also characterize our times and our society.

What is the best explanation for this state of affairs? Why is it that with

1

all our affluence and opportunities, our world ranking on a social problems index is so high? In the American world of intellectual discourse today, there is no shortage of explanations. One is that there has been a decline in religion; it is felt that the enemy is "secular humanism," something that must be rooted out in favor of traditional religious practices. Another is that the rise of the welfare state has sapped our economic motivation as well as our moral strength. We have become a nation of spoiled citizens, waiting for government handouts and unwilling to do a day's work. Partisans of this position feel that great gains can be made by undoing the welfare state, by taking government out of our lives. Then there are those who argue, like Goldsmith, that affluence itself is the cause; the rich always evince depravities from which the poor, in their nobility, are immune. A common answer proferred by those who hold this view is that we turn back the technological clock, and perhaps retreat to the woods with "four acres and independence." Still others believe that the fault lies in the distribution of income; if somehow we could achieve real economic equality our problems would disappear. Egalitarians urge a much more extensive welfare state than we have today. Finally, many would argue that our problems stem from our relatively high population diversity. It is impossible, they maintain, for a nation with so many ethnic and racial groups ever to be a placid and orderly society; the best we can do is to "pull up the gangplank" and prevent the future exacerbation of our current problems.

Each of these explanations is not without plausibility. But it should be pointed out that most have to a rather large degree the character of partisan pleadings of special interest groups; of religionists, of wealthy businessmen, of drop-outs, of civil servants, and of those who feel that their comfort is impeded by the diversity of the population. The answer to the plight of modern civilization is a good bit more complex than any of these explanations suggests.

The purpose of this book is to add to but also to sharpen the intellectual debate about the social problems of contemporary metropolitan life in the United States. My view is that the actions of human beings are to a significant degree shaped by their social surroundings, especially those social relationships in which people through their daily lives are embedded. In this book I explore sociologically the genesis of social problems in the underlying fabric of life in metropolitan communities, the social structures and environments in which most of us lead our everyday lives. Could it be that the very character of the community environments in which we live is a major contributor to our woes?

The study of social problems—their causes, conditions, and consequences—has been the main raison d'être of the discipline of sociology since its inception. Although I have not hesitated to venture far outside the field when necessary, my academic perspective is that of urban sociology. The traditional concern of urban sociology has been the relationship between "settlement patterns" and "social structure," that is, between characteristics of such locality groupings as neighborhoods, towns, cities, and metropolitan areas, and the nature of social life within these groupings.[2] It is this relationship that is explored throughout this work. How does the character of metropolitan communities—social bonds, cultural patterns, population density and scale, modes of transportation and communication, interpersonal networks—affect the everyday lives of metropolitan residents? What are the effects, for example, on family relationships, use of leisure time, and the sense of well-being?

The main thesis developed in the following pages is that life in metropolitan communities has become overly privatized. In our single-minded pursuit of private pleasure we have severely undercut the public ties upon which successful communities depend. As human communities, metropolitan areas are fragmented, amorphous, impersonal, and unsupportive of many basic human endeavors. Although not always obvious, the human consequences of this social condition are a cause for some alarm. To paraphrase Oliver Goldsmith, when communities decay, men decay.

## The Comparative Perspective

The thesis of "community decline" in urban settings has been one of the traditional theses in urban sociology, surrounded by debate and not without its strong academic detractors. A contribution of this study is the cross-cultural exploration of the thesis, and examination of it against the broad canvas of metropolitan life in several different societies. My attempt has been to place the American condition in perspective, to look for both American uniqueness and commonalities between our condition and that of other advanced societies.

Cross-societal comparisons are no longer unfamiliar to most Americans. With a sudden intensity we are looking more to the rest of the world for knowledge, for answers, and even for reassurance. A big focus of attention today, for example, is on the American work environment. Something there seems to be wrong, causing falling productivity and high unemployment. So we are straining our necks to find out what is going on in Japan, where work organizations operate very differently and with apparently far more success.

Yet there is another environment in people's lives, the residential environment, that is at least as important. Indeed, the majority of Americans—men, women, and children—do not work, but they do spend much of the day and all of the night in a residential environment (and those who do work typically value most their time spent at home). If something is wrong with our work environments by the standard of comparison with other countries, perhaps something is wrong with our residential environments as well. Could not our metropolitan areas suffer from a failure of social productivity analogous to the workplace's failure of economic productivity?

The importance of comparative analysis comes quickly into view in a consideration of the traditional explanations mentioned above for the American social malaise, such as the decline of religion, too much affluence, and an excessive welfare state. In the search for evidence to support these explanations, should one not ask at the outset: How does the United States differ in these respects from other advanced societies? A brief survey of the dozen or so societies that make up the world's urban-industrial vanguard would quickly turn up the fact that some have much less religion than we do (Sweden), more welfare state provisions (the Netherlands), greater affluence (Switzerland), more economic insecurity (Great Britain), and a higher population diversity (Belgium). Yet these societies do not have social problems of the magnitude found in the United States. In its problems, and its social conditions, is this society unique in ways that set it quite apart from the rest of the industrialized world? Are we the captive, at an advanced stage, of social trends that will soon overtake every modern society? The only way to find answers to such fundamental questions is through cross-national comparative inquiry.

In a recent article in the *American Journal of Sociology*, Cambridge University sociologist Anthony Giddens issued a "clarion call for a revitalized comparative sociology of advanced societies." "We should abandon the practice, which would in any case scarcely be defended by anyone in principle, of constructing theories of development on the basis of single cases."[3] In this admonition, he is in step with a strong trend toward cross-national comparative studies that can be seen emerging in American sociology today, and that has been in evidence for some years in the European branches of the discipline.

The trend toward cross-national comparative studies represents in some ways a return to the approach that dominated the discipline's founding fathers, especially Max Weber. Indeed, Weber's *The City* (1921), an historical and cross-cultural analysis of urban life, is one of the classics of urban sociology and urban studies. The disciplinary focus of American sociology for much of the twentieth century, in contrast, has been much more narrowly conceived, and the historical and cultural sweep of life and events has largely been put aside. Yet I think it is reasonable to say that the move today toward wider intellectual horizons represents not so much a conscious attempt to return to the vision of the founding fathers as it does a natural evolution of a young discipline. American sociology is beginning to grow beyond its parochialism; as the knowledge of American life becomes ever more refined, the search almost of necessity turns to wider angles of vision. It may be no coincidence that this evolution of a discipline comes at a time when the advanced nations of the world, as never before and despite their many differences, have a growing sense of themselves as a single economic if not also a social and political unity. Certainly they now have a sense that their fate is a common one, one that overrides national differences.

Two societies have been chosen for direct comparison in this book with the United States: Great Britain and Sweden. Although differing in societal scale and in other important respects to be discussed below and in following chapters, these nations, along with the United States, are among the most advanced societies in the world in terms of urban industrialism, that set of social forces that has been the most powerful engine of change in the modern world. If urban-industrial development can be conceived as a unitary and evolutionary process, each of these nations today stands at about the same level of development, albeit there are leads and lags of some significance. Great Britain was the earliest nation to achieve urban-industrial prominence, the world's pioneer in this respect; the United States is the most powerful of the world's urban-industrial societies; and Sweden is probably the world's most successful urban-industrial society, as measured in terms of standard of living as well as the minimization of the negative effects of urban and industrial growth.

In addition to their advanced level of urban industrialism, the three nations are probably the most similar of the advanced societies in basic dimensions of culture and social structure. Each is a highly pragmatic and rational society that emphasizes efficiency and practicality. And each is world renowned for political stability and the practice of democracy, and for the strength of its social and economic institutions. The three societies also bear a striking resemblance in the degree to which their dominant societal goals are economic growth and the advancement of material well-being, but in this respect they are little different from almost all other societies in the world today.

For comparative analysis, however, it is the differences and not the similarities that command one's attention. Sweden is a relatively homogeneous society with a small population, about 8 million, which contrasts with the diverse United States population of 232 million (Britain falls in between, with about 56 million). More important still, in looking at urban-industrial life in these three advanced societies, one is struck immediately by the remarkable differences in the physical setting of their urban and metropolitan areas.

How could three such similar societies, at the same level of urban and industrial development, have evolved urban areas as dissimilar as Stockholm, London, and Chicago (New York is very atypical of the United States), or Gothenburg (Sweden's second city), Liverpool, and Dallas? It does not seem logically to follow from Sweden's great wealth, high rate of automobile ownership (the highest in Europe), and large amount of available land for urban development, that that nation should have what is probably the most compact metropolitan living pattern among Western societies, with most residents living in small apartments and relying on public transportation and other publicly provided services. Wealth, automobiles, and land typically are associated with the United States metropolitan pattern, the most dispersed in the world, where most residents live in single-family, detached houses and rely on private automobiles and a great variety of private services. Nor do the differences in metropolitan setting seem related to the population size difference between the two nations.

One might expect to find Sweden's compact and high-density metropolitan environment in Britain, the tight little island. Instead, the English urban pattern is more American than it is European, with many people living in detached or semidetached houses, and with metropolitan areas built, as a consequence, at relatively low densities. On a range from compact to dispersed metropolitan form, apartment to single-family-house living, and public to private services, Sweden and the United States are at the two extremes, and England is just about in the middle.

Sweden and Great Britain were picked for comparison with the United States, then, because although similar in many fundamental respects, they represent the full range of metropolitan development in advanced societies. Moreover, they express the continuum of Western economic and political systems ranging from relatively free market capitalism to welfare capitalism. (As we shall see, metropolitan development and type of political and economic system are by no means unrelated.)

Especially in the United States, the terms *urban* and *metropolitan* often are associated with the lower—or under—classes and with minority groups. This association is not as strong in the European context. In Sweden, for example, center-city dwellers tend to be considerably wealthier than other members of the society, and until the last few decades, minority groups in Swedish cities did not exist. Partly for reasons of comparability, therefore, I have limited this study to a comparison of the "middle mass" of metropolitan citizens, those who make up the stable working and middle classes. In the United States more than 70 percent of metropolitan residents can be classified as belonging to these classes, and the percentage for the European countries may be even higher. This is not a book on urban poverty or race relations, however important those topics may be. Nor does it dwell very long on the upper-class urbanites in each nation. The latter—residents of Park Avenue, Grosse Point, and Beverly Hills in the United States—may provide a model for many urban dwellers to try to emulate, but it is no more than a model, and one often far removed from the typicality of metropolitan life.

## An Urban Turning Point?

Urban dwellers in advanced societies are currently witnessing what may be a major turning point in urban history. During the 1970s and at first largely unnoticed by ordinary citizen and urban specialist alike, there occurred a significant social event: the decline of the great period of postwar urbanization in advanced societies. This decade saw the termination of the postwar housing shortage in Sweden as the building of apartments finally caught up with demand. It saw the end of New Town building in Britain as the focus of urban development turned back again to central-city areas. And it saw a curtailing of the great, postwar suburban development boom in the United States, to such a degree in fact that some were decrying the loss for most people of the realization of the long-standing American dream of a suburban house.[4]

These events were closely associated with urban demographic changes that were most visible in the United States but were paralleled in the other advanced countries. For the first time in United States history, many of our metropolitan areas stopped growing. The older cities have been losing population for many decades, some since near the turn of the century. And millions of Americans have lived for a while in center cities, only to soon leave for the metropolitan periphery. But never before was there a time in United Sates history when metropolitan areas did not show a larger population at the end of a decade than they had at its beginning.[5]

Not all metropolitan areas are in decline. Areas in the Sunbelt especially are growing almost as fast as ever. Moreover, many new metropolitan areas are in the process of formation. But there is reason to hold, nonetheless, that in the 1970s the United States reached a watershed of urbanization: from being an ever-urbanizing society it evolved into a society in which there was a significant movement of people away from metropolitan areas. In general, the larger the metropolitan area, the steeper was the decline in its population.

Metropolitan development and metropolitan life may in the future be quite different from what they are today. Before the next wave of community building begins it seems essential to think more seriously, based on present and past experience, about how we might want to change the social character of future communities. To do this we first must take careful stock of the social conditions of contemporary metropolitan life.

## The Plan of This Book

Part I begins with a brief review of the historical emergence of metropolitan areas in each nation, emphasizing the immense changes in community life that followed the industrial revolution in England. The remarkable diversity among the metropolitan settings in Sweden, Great Britain, and the United States is discussed in Part II. These settings provide an entree to the social worlds of metropolitan areas. Are the variations in physical setting related to similar variations in metropolitan ways of life and community structure? Are the variations in ways of life and community structure as great, and as significant, as the variations in setting? These are the issues considered in Part III.

In the final part of this book I present an interpretation of life and change in the metropolitan community. Using the materials in Parts II and III as an empirical grounding, I assess metropolitan culture as a whole, emphasizing the social trends that have generated massive privatization together with their human consequences. To conclude, the implications of this analysis for urban social policy in the United States are put forth, with suggested goals for urban community development in the future.

## Notes

1. Lewis Mumford, *The City in History* (New York: Harcourt, Brace & World, 1961), p. 546.
2. See Claude S. Fischer, "On the Marxian Challenge to Urban Sociology," *Comparative Urban Research* 6, nos. 2, 3, (1978): 10-19; and Claude S. Fischer, "The Study of Urban Community and Personality" in *Annual Review of Sociology,* ed. Alex Inkeles et al. (Palo Alto: Annual Review, 1975), pp. 67-89.
3. Anthony Giddens, "Classic Social Theory and the Origins of Modern Sociology" *American Journal of Sociology* 81 (1976): 722.
4. George Sternlieb, "Death of the American Dream House," *Society*, February 1972, pp. 39-42.
5. This trend was first identified in the early 1970s by Calvin Beale of the U.S. Bureau of the Census. For an early statement, see Peter A. Morris and J.P. Wheeler, *Rural Renaissance in America?* (Washington, DC: Population Reference Bureau, 1976).

# PART I
# HISTORY

# 1

# The Rural to Urban Transition

For the first few hundred thousand years of their existence on earth, human beings lived in small groups that seldom exceeded a hundred people. First as roving, hunting bands, then as settled agricultural villages, these groups encapsulated every dimension of life from the material to the spiritual, the personal to the societal.[1] The majority of persons on the globe still live today in small rural groupings, except that their lives are increasingly enmeshed in the larger units of tribe and nation-state. Even in urban societies, the cultural roots in these small, self-contained communities are not far below the surface, embedded, to use Lewis Mumford's phrase, "in birth and place, blood and soil."[2]

People were not able to leave these land-tied groupings until increases in agricultural productivity yielded a surplus sufficient for some to live off the food production of others.[3] The first nonagricultural town dwellers did not emerge until some seven or eight thousand years ago, an event often regarded as synonymous with the rise of civilization. But it was not until less than two hundred years ago, and then only in a handful of nations, that further agricultural advances together with the industrial revolution permitted more than a tiny minority of people to savor the privileges as well as the drawbacks of urban-industrial life.

The mass movement of people from village to town and then to city and metropolitan area, and from farm to factory and later to nonindustrial work organization, is one of the greatest social changes in human history. While still under way in most parts of the world, it is a change that has nearly run its course in the affluent societies of the West, where almost three-quarters of the population live in urban localities and less than 5 percent of the work force are engaged in agriculture. Yet the effects of the great change—in every aspect of society from sex roles to political structure—are still being played out. Explaining the causes of this great social change was the dominant motif of classical sociology; carefully scrutinizing

its effects has been perhaps the principal activity of the following generations of sociologists, including the current one.[4]

The main dimensions of urban-industrial change are almost too well
known to bear repeating. Because several of them are the main substance
of this study, however, and many are not beyond controversy, it is important to outline them as a foundation for further discussion. As in later
chapters, I shall view these changes principally from those perspectives
most relevant to people's everyday lives.

Industrialization can be defined as "the transfer of inanimate energy
sources to the production of goods through the agency of factory organization."[5] It consists of two main components: technological developments,
such as the steam engine and electric power, replacing human effort; and
the organization of production through routinized organization—the factory. In the early industrial revolution industrialism took a capitalist form:
production was oriented to the making of private profit, and was organized
in terms of a market for commodities. Later in history, industrialization
has taken place in many parts of the world under state socialist forms, with
state-owned factories and a government-managed economy.

The industrial revolution began in England in the last few decades of the
eighteenth century. Prior to this time nonagricultural production had
made its way into many villages and many homes; home weavers had
become quite common, for example. But work and home remained united,
few people worked for wages, and village culture and social unity remained
tied to the land and to feudal traditions.

Industrialization radically changed the nature of work. But it just as
radically changed the nature of communities and community life. While
many cities and towns had been in existence before the industrial revolution, devoted to such functions as trade, government, and religion, not
until after the industrial revolution did people leave farms in large numbers and urban communities become the principal form of settlement.
Thus industrialization and urbanization are very closely interlinked, at
least in the experience of the West, and it is accurate to discuss the great
transformations that took place in societies under the heading of the rural
to urban transition.

### The Preindustrial English Village

England represents the first and still the classic case of urban-industrial
development in the West, the case to which all later forms of development
beg to be compared. Accordingly, it will serve our purposes well to develop
in some detail the English experience, and in the next chapter to comment
on the main variations to that experience posed by Sweden and the United

States.[6] For thousands of years, until industrialization began in earnest in the last part of the eighteenth century, England was a nation of small villages. Rooted in the land, and perhaps several hundred people in size,[7] these villages were relatively self-contained minisocieties, organized for hundreds of years prior to the industrial revolution along feudal lines. Originally all village land was owned by the feudal lord of the manor and most villagers were serfs, granted enough land for self-sufficient farming in return for regularly giving to the head of the manor agricultural produce and assisting him in times of war. Over time further social gradations came into being as some serfs became freemen, owning or renting their land for cash; later domestic or cottage industry entered the villages, and the lives of families became divided between farm and workshop. But the society remained tightly bonded by its hierarchial class structure, by the dominance of religion and the church, and by the rhythm of the seasons and the agricultural year.

At heart, each small village was a cluster of households centered on the cultivation of adjacent land. The average household size is estimated by Peter Laslett to have had between four and five persons, but this average masks great variation around the mean.[8] Unlike the situation in most modern societies, household size increased with social status, so wealthy families averaged nine persons per household while very poor families were often only two in number.[9] The larger households of the wealthy are accounted for not only by a larger number of children living at home but also a more extended family network under one roof and a contingent of servants. Servants were common even in the homes of middle-class tradesmen and yeoman farmers.

The villagers lived in cottages and worked within walking distance of their homes. Life was lived always in the company of others, with personal privacy at an absolute minimum. The "others" often as not consisted of substantially the same people throughout life, varying mainly through births and deaths. The village was an almost self-contained unit, a society in miniature, that encapsulated the lives of its residents. It contained a society of rich and poor, young and old, all in daily contact and living within visual distance of one another. Although there was contact with neighboring villages and towns, and some social mobility among them, the great majority of people probably lived out their lives in the villages in which they were born. For better and for worse, each village consisted of a small number of sequestered people forced to share a common life together within a limited space. "To the facts of geography, being together in one place," as Laslett notes in *The World We Have Lost*, "were added all the bonds which are forged between human beings when they permanently are alongside each other; bonds of intermarriage and of kinship, of common ancestry and common experience and of friendship and cooperation in matters of common concern."[10]

While this basic social structure in which the majority of English people lived for millennia is quite clear, our knowledge of the "feel" of these communities is much more cloudy and subject to speculation. Moreover, comparisons with modern communities are made extremely difficult due to the vast transformations that have taken place in every other social and cultural sphere. Materially, it is probably a reasonable generalization that life was "nasty, brutish and short." Certainly this must have been the case for most English villages prior to the Elizabethan renaissance in the 1500s. As W.G. Hoskins notes, "In 1550 most English people were still living in the rather dark, squalid and cramped dwellings of their medieval forefathers. These were generally two roomed houses—a hall and bower—built of a timber frame with walls of reinforced mud, the whole raised upon a rubble foundation. There were no glazed windows."[11] None of these dwellings survives to this day.

Life expectancy at birth in preindustrial England was no more than thirty to forty years, lower than that in the poorest Third World nations today.[12] There was no great fear in England of foreign invasions, but life was constantly threatened by illness, pestilence, and economic downturn, and there was a continuing personal as well as collective fight for survival.

In social feel, however, life in the preindustrial English village was as different from the modern scene as in material level. Family relationships were extraordinarily cohesive, and often must have provided a powerful emotional anchorage in a turbulent world. Again in the words of Peter Laslett, "Time was when the whole of life went forward in the family, in a circle of loved, familiar faces, known and fondled objects, all to human size."[13]

This is not to suggest that medieval family life was any more "loving" than such life in the present day. Intensity of human relationships can breed enmity as well as love. Moreover, the evidence is fairly clear that medieval childhood was, in the language of Lloyd de Mause, "a nightmare from which we have only recently begun to awaken."[14] It is all too easy to romanticize about medieval life, to fall into the pattern of thinking that Henry Adams did in *Mont Saint-Michel and Chartres*, for example, and for which he has been so roundly criticized.[15] Indeed, recent "firsthand" accounts of medieval life that have been uncovered, such as Le Roy Ladurie's *Montaillou*, cast serious doubt on the idea that these times were marked by any special nobility or virtue.[16] But one can say with some certainty that life took place for the most part in a very close-knit family— a small circle of intensely loyal members who felt a deep sense of sharing a common fate in the struggle for survival.

In addition, the collected families in a single settlement were enmeshed together through the necessity for communal effort with what was probably a deep sense of communal loyality.[17] The necessities of rural life, for example ploughing, harvesting, and barn raising, required recurrent cooperative activity among families that has no parallel today. Like the members of a single family, community residents were also imbued with a strong sense of sharing a common fate. This intense "sense of community" rested on the community's being a single economic enterprise, a phenomenon quite foreign to the urban scene. Moreover, as often as not the individual household was the scene of economic labor, a very far cry from the strict separation of residence and work that is universal in urban-industrial settings.

Again, one must be careful not to exaggerate the positive social character of medieval village life. The English villages were the scene of profound exploitation of the poor by the rich, of younger by elder siblings, and of a pervading patriarchy that placed women in a form of servitude that today would be judged intolerable. For what it is worth, however, many of these may not have been strongly felt injustices, in the sense that we think of them today: people tended to accept their lot in life. Medieval life was, after all, relatively immutable and there was little expectation of reform.

## The Coming of Industry

The earliest forms of industrialization did little to upset the primitive symmetry of the English rural village. Water mills for grinding corn, for example, had been a part of the English landscape since the eighth century. In medieval Lincolnshire, it is estimated, one village in three contained such a mill.[18] Other highly decentralized industrial developments blended into the English rural scene, both in function and in appearance, in ways that were not appreciably upsetting to the rural way of life. Such developments include small-scale mines, quarries, and coal pits, salt works, and glass works. Even the early "factories"—typically cottage industries making textiles—were extensions of the household, which had always been the scene of substantial economic activity.

The massive shift in community life came only after the development of larger-scale factories that required the assemblage of a sizable labor force at sites far beyond the confines of agricultural jurisdictions. Because they were based on water power, as in the case of Alexander Darby's iron mill at Coalbrookdale (1760), Josiah Wedgewood's pottery plant at Etruria (1769), and Arkwright's textile mill at Cromford (1771), even these factories were at first located in rural settings, "close to the land," often in remote river valleys. These early factories produced at best small hamlets or villages not too different in scale from their rural counterparts. That these new environments were not too inhuman and distorted is attested to by the fact that the factory owners, as in the case of Darby and Wedgewood, lived right next door to their workplaces, their homes providing a vantage point from which they could continuously oversee and view their creation with pride.

All of this changed with the introduction of an extremely consequential new form of energy, steam power—the steam engine fed by coal. Although it has been estimated that more than three hundred steam engines were built between 1775 and 1800,[19] it was not until the early part of the nineteenth century that use of the steam engine burgeoned, and a major development occurred that led to the industrial city. Freed from the necessity of being beside a fast-flowing river, factories organized around the steam engine sought flat land in open country, often in the vicinity of major coalfields. In the rush for competitive profits, workers' housing was thrown up quickly, cheaply, and haphazardly, and it was not long before Charles Dickens's "Coketowns" came to dominate the English landscape. As Lewis Mumford has pointedly stated, early industrialism "produced the most degraded urban environment the world had yet seen; for even the quarters of the ruling classes were befouled and overcrowded."[20] It should be noted that it was not long before the factory owners fled, distancing themselves in residential locations that were to become choice suburban areas.

Towns and one large city, London, had of course been prominent features of the English scene for centuries prior to the industrial revolution. Especially in the late Middle Ages, England saw a growth of towns that soaked up some of the excess rural population and spawned a small middle class. But in the late seventeenth century less than a quarter of the English people lived in towns and cities (more than a third of these made up London's population of slightly more than half a million), and the average town dweller lived in a settlement of less than a thousand persons.[21] Moreover, most towns were trading or market places, not industrial sites. They formed a network whose main function, it can be said without too much exaggeration, was to supply rural produce to London. Many of these old market towns became the locus of industrial cities, and during the eighteenth century they helplessly saw their population balloon and their character change.

The rapid growth of urban development, both around existing market towns and on virgin land, was not solely the result of new energy technologies. It also stemmed from new agricultural technologies generating a higher crop yield on a given amount of land; from significant improvements in transportation; and from a rapid increase in the English population that was the result, more than anything else, of a lowering of the death rate. Each of these factors generated a migration from the villages, and eventually a breakdown in the old village way of life, culminating in England's status as the first urbanized society.

The village way of life was further destroyed by the enclosure of land, especially that ordered by Acts of Parliament from the 1750s onward. Village fields that for centuries had been "held in common," and collectively tilled and grazed, became "enclosed," that is, taken over by private ownership and often hedged or fenced in. The economic gains from the enclosure movement were very real, especially through the greater acceptance of new agricultural technologies and production methods. But, as G.M. Trevelyan notes, "The social price paid for economic gain was a decline in the number of independent cultivators and a rise in the number of landless laborers."[22] Over time the village farm population drastically eroded, resulting eventually in most villages becoming the spill-over residences for the new industrial poor and, at a still later stage, habitats for both urban retirees and wealthier urbanites fleeing from the cities in search of tranquility and nostalgia.[23]

Thus in a relatively short period the residential environment and related way of life of the typical English person underwent a quite drastic and radical change. The suddenness of this mass change can easily be overemphasized. Traditional village life, after all, had begun to corrode long before the industrial revolution. And the urban way of life did not spring full blown overnight. But the very radical character of the social change for the average person can in no way be denied.

### The Early Industrial Cities

Perhaps the major factor dictating the environmental character of the early industrial town, once the factories had been geographically located with reference to their needs for resources and for transportation, was the economic necessity to cluster large numbers of workers within walking distance of the factories. This caused the construction of housing at densities far greater than those in most urban places up to that time, to say nothing of the villages from which the workers came. And while the housing was of very poor quality, basic public services like water, waste disposal, and health care were even worse and sometimes nonexistent. Moreover, the villagers who migrated to the city were from the lowest economic stratum, and typically lacked the social and technical skills necessary for coping with urban life.

This combination of factors in the industrial cities of England during the nineteenth century often generated a kind of social sink. Despite the tremendous growth of jobs and income, some observers believe that the standard of living of the villagers-turned-urban-dwellers actually remained the same or even declined over the decades. "In half a century of the fullest development of industrialism," states E.P. Thompson, "the standard of living still remained—for very large but indeterminate groups—at the point of subsistency."[24] Nevertheless, we now know that the forces then set in motion led to the greatest material affluence, both in amount and in distribution, that world societies have ever experienced or even thought possible.

In their physical form and outward appearance the early English cities and towns were more medieval than modern.[25] This was due largely to their pedestrian nature; the means of mass urban transportation remained at a very primitive level of development. Urban structure was cellular rather than being functionally differentiated: each of many similar areas had a jumbled combination of uses—for living, working, and shopping— in a way quite distinct from today's metropolis. In addition, there was very little overall centrality. Rather than a dominant central business district with tall buildings, a form that was generated by the introduction of the trolley and the railroad, business districts were scattered throughout the urban area so as to be within walking distance of homes. The same pattern held true for factories and other places of work.

But our main concern is with the actual changes in community and way of life that urban industrialism had brought forth. The list of such changes can be virtually limitless, and we will comment here only on those main changes that had a tangible effect on people's daily lives. It is usual to start with changes in the nature of work, for in many scholarly circles, even those that are non-Marxist, the economic dimension of one's existence is regarded as the "prime mover."

Work in the industrial city gradually ceased to be a family affair. The lone worker (sometimes including women and children) would go off each day to a factory at some distance. At the factory, work was no longer conducted alongside family and kinfolk but often in the presence of strangers, and the work was organized in terms of large and impersonal groupings operated along bureaucratic lines, something totally absent in village life.[26]

At night the worker returned to a home that became only a domicile and no longer a place of productive activity. From being the center of life the home was to become a refuge from life, a place where one could find not social activity but privacy and repose. Because the family, including the extended family, lost so many economic functions, familial relationships and ties to relatives changed greatly in character, becoming less binding and more voluntary.

Due to the changes in both work and family, the situation of women altered markedly. Although the village society was one of male authoritarianism, the village economy typically was based on an equal economic partnership between husband and wife; the economy depended on the labor of both partners in each household. The industrial revolution initially may have given some women the option of working for wages outside the confines of the household, a development that is usually regarded as "liberating," but eventually the industrial system was to put married women (especially in the middle class) into a position of great economic dependence—housewife.[27] While housewives maintained power over their traditional domain, the home, and even had more time for such functions as child rearing, their domain had shrunk seriously in activity and in economic importance, leaving many women in an off-center position in life. This position of women—economically dependent, politically impotent, and socially cut off—continued up to the present century, when a declining family size, a changing economy, and a rising women's movement's demands for equality have changed the picture somewhat. But there is as yet no advanced society where women even approach the level of economic equality between the sexes found in the village household economy, however many other egalitarian gains women may have achieved.

Perhaps the most far-reaching as well as overlooked social change that stemmed from the industrial revolution was the change in local community life. Whereas the village community had a collective identity and even a measure of collective action, the urban-industrial community was to become merely a place to live and work, a place in which there was very little collective identity (except initially in small neighborhood groupings) and where collective action was only grudgingly tolerated, and then mainly through elected representatives. The industrial city no longer was a specialized economy in which all must participate in the pressing fight for survival.

Nor was the city any longer a social grouping on a scale at which "everyone could know everyone else." One's public life in the city came to be characterized by an anonymity that was wholly foreign to the villager: a very large number of persons encountered during a typical day, even if only briefly and in passing, were strangers, persons for whom one held at best only abstract and generalized feelings of comradeship.

A community of strangers, especially when those strangers come from very different rural traditions, demands an entirely different social fabric than a community of intimates. Intimates are able to socialize the young to group norms and to enforce conformity to those norms through a wide variety of informal processes, ranging from a nod of the head to social ostracism. A community of strangers not only finds difficulty in agreeing on what norms should be followed but also no longer can rely on the natural and spontaneous actions of all community members to enforce those norms; it must rely instead on persons who are specially trained for that purpose, such as police, judges, and educators. Thus the character of the community as a whole takes on many of the same qualities found in the industrial workplace: impersonality, specialization, and bureaucratic organization.[28]

Community ties were weakened still further through the rising social and geographic mobility that accompanied industrial development. People no longer lived their lives in a single community and in the presence of a single set of people. Capitalism demanded a highly mobile labor force, and residential mobility became quite common even after the primal move from village to town. Empirical sociological research of the present day has concluded that nothing disrupts a sense of community identity and attachment so much as residential mobility, and that must surely have been as true in the early days of industrialism.[29]

These changes in work, home, and community were not sudden; they took place very gradually over decades and even centuries. The early industrial cities, as indeed some areas of cities even today in advanced societies, had many of the earmarks of village life. Sometimes urban quarters became the transplanted locales for persons from a single village or group of adjacent villages, and these quarters could be maintained with a high degree of insulation from the surrounding urban environment. Moreover, it was not uncommon for the household economy to persevere at the interstices of urban life.

In addition, rural villages can still be found even in the most advanced societies, however much their life-styles may be compromised by the invasions of an otherwise urbanized society and culture. Yet the trends discussed here do seem to have an inevitability, an inexorable quality that suggests that the more affluent and "advanced" a society, the more the trends will become manifest. The way they manifest themselves in advanced societies today is precisely the theme of later chapters in this book.

We have gone into some detail about the social structure of the early English rural village because it provides a marvelous image with which to compare the social structure of community life today. It is appropriate again at this point, however, to warn the reader that in our single-minded focus on village life, and on the structural changes in the relations of work, home, and community that followed the industrial revolution, we do not pretend to be giving a balanced view of "modernization" as a whole.[30] That these community changes are associated with massive increases in social efficiency, political democracy, personal affluence, education and knowledge, and perhaps even sociocultural "rationality" must continuously be kept in mind.

### Notes

1. See Lionel Tiger and Robin Fox, *The Imperial Animal* (New York: Holt, Rinehart & Winston, 1971).
2. Lewis Mumford, *The City in History* (New York: Harcourt Brace & World, 1961), p. 14.

3. V. Gordon Childe, *Man Makes Himself* (New York: Mentor Books, 1951).
4. See Robert Nisbet, *The Sociological Tradition* (New York: Basic Books, 1966).
5. Anthony Giddens, *The Class Structure of Advanced Societies* (London: Hutchinson, 1973), p. 141.
6. I shall concentrate this historical discussion on England, rather than Wales or Scotland; there are differences among these areas, but to develop them here would take us far afield.
7. Peter Laslett, *The World We Have Lost* (New York: Scribner's, 1971), p. 56.
8. Ibid., p. 66.
9. Ibid., p. 67.
10. Ibid., p. 81.
11. W.G. Haskins, *The Making of the English Landscape* (Baltimore: Penguin Books, 1955), p. 155.
12. E.A. Wrigley, *Population and History* (New York: World University Library, 1969).
13. Laslett, *The World We Have Lost*, p. 22.
14. Lloyd de Mause, *The History of Childhood* (New York: Psychohistory Press, 1974), p. 1. For other negative views of the emotional climate of traditional family life, see Edward Shorter, *The Making of the Modern Family* (New York: Basic Books, 1975); and Philippe Ariès, *Centuries of Childhood* (New York: Random House, 1962).
15. Henry Adams, *Mont Saint-Michel and Chartres* (Garden City, New York: Doubleday/Anchor, 1959; first published 1905).
16. Le Roy Ladurie, *Montaillou* (New York: George Braziller, 1978).
17. See Laslett, *The World We Have Lost*, ch. 3.
18. Haskins, *Making of the English Landscape*, p.80.
19. Ibid., p. 224.
20. Mumford, *City in History*, p. 447.
21. Laslett, *The World We Have Lost*, pp. 57, 58.
22. G.M. Trevelyan, *English Social History* (Baltimore: Penguin Books, 1977), p. 394.
23. Peter Ambrose, *The Quiet Revolution* (Sussex: Sussex University Press, 1974).
24. E.P. Thompson, *The Making of the English Working Class* (Baltimore: Penguin Books, 1977), p. 229.
25. See Gideon Sjoberg, *The Pre-Industrial City* (New York: Free Press, 1960); and D.I. Scargill, *The Form of Cities* (London: Bell & Hyman, 1979).
26. See Louise A. Tilly and Joan W. Smith, *Women, Work and Family* (New York: Holt, Rinehart & Winston, 1978); and Neil J. Smelser, *Social Change in the Industrial Revolution* (Chicago: University of Chicago Press, 1959).
27. See Ann Oakley, *Women's Work: The Housewife, Past and Present* (New York: Pantheon Books, 1974).
28. Although marred by excessive and sometimes questionable abstractions, the classic work on community change was *Gemeinschaft und Gesellschaft* by Ferdinand Toennies, first published in 1887. The book was translated into English by C.P. Loomis: *Fundamental Concepts of Sociology* (New York: American Book Company, 1940).
29. John D. Kasarda and Morris Janowitz, "Community Attachment in Mass Society," *American Sociological Review* 39 (July 1974).
30. A recent and excellent review of modernization theory is Wilbert E. Moore, *World Modernization* (New York: Elsevier, 1979).

# 2

# The Path to Metropolitan Life

## Urban Development in England since the Industrial Revolution

The early industrial cities and towns were but one step in England's evolution to a fully urbanized, metropolitan society. Throughout the first three-quarters of the nineteenth century housing densities rose in cities to unparalleled heights, a result of the fundamental necessity for workers to be able to get back and forth between home and work twice during the day (including the trip home for lunch). At the same time, however, municipal reforms enacted by Parliament eased somewhat the terrible sanitary and public health conditions and set minimum standards for urban housing development. And some of the new industrial wealth of England found its way into better municipal services.[1]

For many decades the first industrial towns and cities maintained much of their medieval cellular pattern: housing clustered densely around scattered factory sites, with a very truncated central business district. The year 1870 marked a turning point. At about that time, and in the years to come, the installation of cheap and efficient public transportation was to alter irrevocably the urban pattern. Hard upon earlier horse-drawn trams, came trams, trolleys, and railroads fueled by steam and electricity, and finally the gasoline-powered buses and automobiles of the twentieth century. Each of these technological developments signaled both the centralization of urban development and its outward spread into the countryside.[2]

By permitting people to live farther from their jobs, the new forms of transportation notably increased the geographic area of the cities and at the same time lowered the densities. The people most likely to make use of the transportation and move to the new "suburbs" were the wealthy and the middle classes, people who had at the same time a strongly felt need to flee the city, and its noxious conditions, for the cleaner air of the countryside. But it was not long before they were followed by some industrial workers,

23

often enticed by low-cost workers' housing built in outlying areas and tied to the development of railroad and commuter lines.

Most commuter lines had as their terminal point the central railroad station, which in turn became a magnet for central-city commercial and office development. Thereby was set in motion the downtown skyscraper complexes of our own day, with, in many advanced nations, ever-diminishing densities as one moves to the urban periphery. As the business districts expanded they necessarily displaced the adjacent residents, consisting in part of the rich, who moved to the suburbs, and later of the poor, who moved into adjacent areas that were to become the twentieth-century slums and "areas of transition." Thus the late nineteenth-century industrial city became a reality, with a strong central business district surrounded by housing for the poor (some rich areas also remained). This was followed concentrically by the vast tracts of working-class housing, often still near to a factory (factories also, however, were beginning to disperse outwardly), and finally the middle-class suburbs and country estates of the very wealthy.[3]

This is still largely the urban form of most English cities, and of cities in other advanced societies built during the same period.[4] But there was another evolutionary stage of development to come, a stage that has more nearly been reached in some other countries, especially the United States, than it has in England itself.

The twentieth century saw the widespread dissemination of technological developments in two spheres that have had massive ramifications for city life: private transportation (the automobile) and mass communications (radio, telephone, television). Until the twentieth century much of urban development had been centripetal in flow, with people pouring into cities, and cities gaining in size, density, and centrality. The automobile and mass communications unleashed centrifugal tendencies that led to the metropolitan areas of our own time—huge masses of people thinly spread over the landscape and only loosely connected to an urban center, a center that itself undergoes continuous, relative decline. As people get far enough from the city center, new subcenters on the urban periphery emerge, both for work and for shopping, and the ties to the center city of the peripheral metropolitan dwellers may be gone forever.

The centrifugal tendencies triggered by technological changes have been aided and abetted by the great personal wealth of advanced societies. This wealth has permitted the widespread use of expensive, high-speed private transportation, and accelerated the demand for larger amounts of private living space. One additional factor of great importance in metropolitan growth was a change in the industrial production process itself that led to the necessity for increasingly large amounts of horizontal factory space, a change that forced industries to seek more outlying locations where land prices were lower.

While each of the three advanced societies to which we are giving special attention has been subject to all of these forces and tendencies of metropolitan development, the patterns that have arisen in each nation are actually quite remarkable for their dissimilarities. The nature of these metropolitan differences, and the causes of them, are the subjects of the next few chapters. By way of introduction, a brief history of urban development in Sweden and the United States is presented here.

## The Different Paths to Metropolitan Life
## in the United States and Sweden

As the world's first urban nation, England was almost fully urbanized by the turn of the twentieth century. By that time some 80 percent of the English population found themselves living in urban areas, and there has been little change in the figure up to the present day. In contrast, both the United States and Sweden urbanized mostly in this century, and perhaps more than anything else this difference in timing explains the divergent character of their urban development.

*Sweden*

Sweden's emergence as a nation of urban dwellers has been the most rapid, and the least problematic, of probably any nation in the world. Industrialization came very late to Sweden compared to Britain and to the principal continental countries. In the late nineteenth and early twentieth centuries Sweden was one of the poorest countries in Europe, a major reason that nearly one-quarter of the Swedish population emigrated to other countries, especially the United States. Still in the 1880s more than three-quarters of the Swedish population were living on farms (compared to about one half of the United States population).[5] Yet by 1930, only a little more than one generation later, Sweden had achieved a parity with England and the United States in her urban and industrial maturity.

The lateness of Swedish industrialization proved to be a boon. With the early industrial experiences of other nations available for close scrutiny, the Swedes were able in large part to avoid many of the negative consequences, suffered especially by England. For example, the Swedes relied much less than the English on the free market, turning instead to government assistance, planning, and control in such matters as the layout of railway lines and other transportation facilities, and the provision of adequate housing and other urban services when new industrial plants were constructed. Also, much municipal land was purchased by local governments and remained under public ownership.[6] Thus counterparts of the shoddy, ill-constructed early industrial towns of England never came to mar the Swedish landscape.

In addition, Sweden profited by entering the industrial scene at a time when the steam engine, with its need for a large agglomeration of workers in often less desirable areas, such as proximity to coalfields, was supplanted by electricity as an energy source that lent itself to a much more decentralized industrial pattern. Electricity enabled much of Swedish industry to be located in the "back woods," in small industrial towns that were close in geography and spirit to the rural scene. This decentralization of industry was enhanced by a government-planned rail network that was designed for accessibility to small and relatively remote places.[7]

One major social consequence of this urban-industrial pattern was that the move to the city on the part of Swedish country people took place in a much more stepwise fashion than in England, with Swedish farmers moving first to very small and nearby industrial villages, and then to progressively larger settlements until the metropolis was reached. This provided the time for the gradual urbanization of the population in the cultural sense, and mitigated the wrenching sociocultural upheaval associated with the prototypical rural-to-urban transition. Moreover, Swedes today continue to live in urban communities of considerably smaller scale than do the urbanites of England or the United States. Three of the six metropolitan areas in Sweden barely meet the standard of "an area of 100,000 or more inhabitants," and nearly half of all settlements in Sweden that are classified as "urban" have between 200 and 499 inhabitants![8]

Finally, the relative placidity of Sweden's rural-to-urban transition was fostered by that nation's sudden rise from poverty to a position of great wealth. It so happened that Sweden had precisely those natural resources, such as iron ore and wood products, that were highly coveted by the more advanced industrial nations. The wealth stemming from the international sale of these resources could then be injected into public services in the new urban-industrial centers, as well as into the continued development of a strong industrial base.[9]

Each of these factors, then—late industrialization and the use of electric power, government planning and control, the emigration of Sweden's surplus labor to other nations, and the rapid accumulation of great wealth—prevented Sweden from the kind of "overurbanization" so commonly found in other urban and industrializing societies. *Overurbanization* means the movement of people to cities at a rate faster than the economy, and the network of urban services, can provide them with a reasonable level of support.

It was only after Sweden had become a relatively mature urban and industrial society that the Social Democrat-controlled government of Sweden, beginning in the early 1930s, developed the massive set of government programs that we now refer to as the welfare state. One does not need to be wholly sympathetic with the Swedish welfare state to hold that this form of government intervention had moderated many of the new social problems to which urban industrialism gave rise.[10] But it also must be realized that the task of the Swedish welfare state was made much less onerous due to the highly successful outcome of the original rural-to-urban transition.

Several additional characteristics of Sweden on its path to metropolitan life must be noted. Sweden never had a fully developed medieval social system marked by serfdom, as did most of the other European countries. As a consequence, more of the Swedish population from an early period consisted of yeomen or independent farmers, and there prevailed in Sweden a relatively strong egalitarianism that permitted an early move to political democracy. Egalitarianism still heavily infuses Swedish life today; Sweden is clearly less "class bound" than England and virtually every continental nation.[11] The comparatively benign nature of Swedish social stratification has undoubtedly played a role in the smooth and extensive development of welfare state programs, many of which required, at the community as well as national levels, a collective approval and action that have not been so easy to generate in other Western nations.

The classic medieval rural village described in the last chapter did exist for centuries in Sweden, but its eventual breakup took a different course than in England. In both England and Sweden the enclosure movements of the eighteenth century had a profound effect on village life. But in England the enclosures did little to break up the physical character of the village; they merely channeled growth elsewhere, and it is still rare in England to find the isolated farmstead on the open fields between villages. Those persons who remained in farming after the enclosures continued to live in the villages and walk to their fields, rather than moving their place of residence. In Sweden, on the other hand, the villages were physically broken apart by the enclosures, and Sweden assumed the rural pattern so commonly seen in the United States: isolated farmsteads scattered across the rural landscape. It was only in the central Swedish province of Dalarna where this breakup of the medieval village did not take place, and that province remains to this day a "folk capital" of Sweden where some villages can still be seen in roughly their original medieval form.[12]

Although the exact nature of the social and cultural impact of the enclosure movement in Sweden is far from clear, the intense community ties discussed with reference to England surely must have been sharply curtailed, giving way to a social as well as physical independence not common to England or to the continental countries (where villages also tended to remain intact). Cut off from some of the supportive ties of village life, the Swedish family unit may even have gained resilience through having to face life more on its own. In any event, far more commonly in Sweden than in England the early town dwellers came not from an intense village life but from an independent homestead. As we shall see, this was also a dominant characteristic of the American rural-to-urban transition.

The new Swedish urban dwellers not only came from different communal environments than their English counterparts but ended up in quite dissimilar settings as well. In its nascent urban residential development Sweden followed closely the English and United States patterns of low-density housing, but early in this century shifted abruptly to the continental pattern of high-density residential areas made up of large apartment blocks even in smaller towns. Now we are intruding on the subject of the following two chapters, however. Suffice it to say here that in Sweden, unlike in the other two countries, it is very common for the new urban dweller to have made the very radical move from the freedom and independence of a relatively isolated and self-owned homestead to the dependence and loss of autonomy associated with life in a high-density rental apartment.

## The United States

In certain basic dimensions the United States differs significantly from its European allies, and it is well to be very clear about those dimensions, however obvious or well known they may be. First, the United States is much larger than the other two nations, both in geographic scale and in population size. The geographic scale has given the United States an expansiveness and freedom not found in Europe; there are many places in the United States, for example, where one can go to "get away from it all," even to put civilization behind. And population size (together with abundant resources) has granted the United States in this century a position of world power not attainable by the other nations (perhaps also a self-centeredness and even arrogance that is not common to the European scene).

American society has no feudal past, save for the cultural norms carried in the minds of immigrants. Indeed, it is fair to say that the United States has no past at all in the European sense. Each new settlement was carved de novo out of the wilderness, a minisociety with a mix of old customs but adapted to new circumstances. This provided the opportunity for great social experimentation and diversity, a diversity that was accentuated still further through the arrival and blending of large immigrant groups from many of the world's societies.

Moreover, the United States has always been a much more mobile society than those of Europe, a mobility that does not seem to have slackened until the last few decades. It was entirely possible for people to abandon their problems in one community and move elsewhere; indeed, that is how most of the nation was settled. As a result of this experience, together with the vastness of United States geography and resources, Americans have always had a more "throw-away" attitude toward their land, natural resources, and even built environment than is found in Europe. Unlike Americans, Europeans have never had the same opportunities to escape from problems through flight (except through emigration to an entirely different society).

The rural-urban transition in the United States has been associated with population movements that were much more extensive than those of England and Sweden. Urbanization has involved long-distance interregional shifts of people: east to west, south to north, and more recently, from the nation's midlands to coastal areas. These movements have often carried people very far from their childhood homes, sometimes intensifying rural-to-urban dislocations that can be severe in even the best of circumstances.

Partly because of the necessity to open up virgin lands, and also owing to the difficulties of establishing new communities, Americans throughout much of their history have been preeminently yeoman farmers living independently on relatively isolated farmsteads. There are few other societies in the world where agriculturalists have been so widely scattered on separate parcels of land, and so removed from communal ties. This historical characteristic undoubtedly leaves its residue in the very relaxed communal ties found in contemporary United States metropolitan areas, ties that seem more oriented to rural individualism than to urban interdependence.

Yet by no means have all Americans lived under the conditions of rural individualism and those who have were typically buffered by a large family and by devout religious ties that often made up for the distances between neighbors. It is easy to overemphasize the theme of individualism in American historical life. Americans also have a communal past that is very real in cultural spirit and tradition if not always in the way in which most Americans have lived.[13] The early settlements of New England were profoundly communal in character, so profound that the individualism that later came to dominate American life was virtually nonexistent. As one scholar has recently noted, "A broadly diffused desire for consensual communalism [was] the operative premise of group life" in the small New England town.[14] And this premise provided the main thread of life for most citizens of New England until nearly the end of the eighteenth century. As in the case of European medieval communities of which they were direct lineal descendants, New England village life had strong aspects of cultural totalitarianism, especially in matters of religion. But it also shared with the medieval village the traits of intense familism, a deep sense of community identity, and the capacity for effective communal action.[15]

This rich communalism was not easily transplanted, and the new communities of the frontier were not able to come close to the binding ties of their predecessors. Yet through most of its history the United States has been a nation of small-town dwellers, with even the independent farmers having significant social ties to the nearby small village or town. And no cultural tradition has loomed larger in the settlement and development of American small towns, especially in the midwestern heartland, than the early New England experience. In architecture, if less so in social relations, the midwestern villages and small towns were very often self-conscious look-alikes of their New England antecedents, with the tall, white church steeple providing the community focal point, next to it the village park or green surrounded by such municipal buildings as the town hall and the school, followed by the neat rows of white clapboard houses on orderly, tree-lined streets.[16] As often as not it is from such an environment that Americans have moved to the new cities and metropolitan areas, and more often than not it is to such an environment that metropolitan Americans today wish to return.

Early industrialism, that which took place prior to the Civil War, provided many parts of the nation with what is now viewed as something of a golden age, and it is instructive to reflect upon that time. The first factories were small and blended into the rural and village landscapes, greatly lifting the standard of living while not unduly upsetting the symmetry of country life. Communities remained closeknit, and the excesses of competitive capitalism were yet to wreak their havoc upon the land. Anthony Wallace describes Rockdale, a small industrial town outside Philadelphia, around 1850:

> In that brief period the dream of an "American System" of manufactures, a harmony of rural and industrial interests and lifeways, nearly became a reality. . . . The Rockdale manufacturing district was almost a self-sufficient rural community, like a plantation or a commune, tied economically to world markets and financial centers by the buying of raw cotton and the selling of yarn and cloth, and linked intellectually and spiritually to the wider culture by the participation of its citizens in migration, travel, and reading. Its social structure of caste and class, its style of family life, were for the moment not seriously in question.[17]

It was during this pre–Civil War period, principally in the decade of the 1840s, that a stable and rich community life in the new nation seemed with great success to have made the transition to the virgin land, with a cultural unanimity on the necessity for, and even uplifting value of, hard work, but hard work tempered by a belief in the family, in education, and in religion. There also was a flourishing of art and thought at this time, especially through the literature of Emerson, Hawthorne, Thoreau, Melville, and

Poe, the main theme of which was an individualism tempered by community responsibility.[18]

The cities of the time presented a different face. In 1850 only 6 percent of Americans lived in urban areas having populations of over 100,000, New York and Philadelphia being in the dominant position with populations of 600,000 and 408,000 respectively, followed by Baltimore and Boston in the 100,000-200,000 range. The social conditions in cities contrasted sharply with the relative tranquillity of small places, and the differential clearly helped to accentuate a strong antiurban temperament that already was a fixed feature in the American mind at the time of the Revolution—notably through the views of Thomas Jefferson—and that remains a prominent feature of American culture to the present day.[19] The manifest antiurbanism of the rural and small-town masses was expressed and fostered by remarks of intellectuals, such as the half-serious one of Nathaniel Hawthorne, that "all towns should be made capable of purification by fire, or of decay, within each half century,"[20] or Emerson's, "that he shuddered when he approached New York."[21] As an "objective" outside observer, de Tocqueville also fanned the antiurban flames when he wrote in 1835, "I look upon the size of certain American cities, and especially on the nature of their population, as a real danger which threatens the future security of the democratic republics of the New World."[22]

There is no convincing evidence that social conditions in American cities during the industrializing period were worse than those in Europe; indeed, they were probably much superior. But it is a reasonable generalization that the conditions—especially the material conditions—in the small towns and countryside were much better than those in their European counterparts, and the contrast helped to magnify the negative side of American urban life. Today, of course, and the situation has prevailed for much of the present century, U.S. cities have a considerably more serious set of difficulties than do those of Europe, including crime, poverty, and slums. Thus the antiurban temperament continues to be fed, even among those whose lives are now inextricably linked to large urban centers. Antiurbanism is by no means only an American phenomenon, however; it is also an issue in Europe, as will be brought out in the chapters to follow.

As noted above, the rapid growth of cities took place in the United States at a much later time than in England. When England was almost fully urbanized, at the turn of the twentieth century, the population of urban places in the United States was only about 40 percent; it was not until after World War I that the U.S. urban population reached a statistical majority. Massive industrialization did not occur until after the Civil War, and was particularly marked in the 1880s.[23] Like Sweden's and in contrast to England's the later industrialization in the United States provided the opportunity for a more decentralized urban-industrial network, an opportunity that often was a necessity as Americans pushed westward into unsettled territory. This decentralization enabled the United States to be essentially a small-town society until well into the twentieth century.

The twentieth-century metropolitan form of urban development, spread cities with weak centers and geared to advanced technology, has flourished more in the United States than in any other nation, especially in the American West and the new South. Built on open land at a time when the appropriate technologies had become available, metropolitan areas like Los Angeles and Houston have scarcely experienced the nineteenth-century urban-industrial form of strong centrality and concentric zones, to say nothing of the early industrial environment oriented to the pedestrian. Particularly significant on the American metropolitan scene are the automobile, the vast interlinking freeway system, and the single-family, detached house. These environmental elements, made possible by our private affluence as much as by our available land area, set the United States apart from most other highly urbanized nations.

### The Path to Metropolitan Life: Summary and Perspectives

The historical, geographic, and cultural dissimilarities of urban life among these three nations are indeed of real consequence for their people and the problems they face. These dissimilarities are explored in much more detail in later chapters. From a broader perspective, however, one that compares metropolitan community life in advanced societies with the life that preceded it, or with the life that still exists in nonmetropolitan areas throughout the world, it is the similarities that are brought to our attention. About 75 percent of the citizens in each of these nations live today in metropolitan communities, historically unique communities that no one planned and few foresaw, and that from a broad comparative perspective share many characteristics. What are these characteristics, and how do they differ from prior community forms? Those are the questions now to be addressed, while at the same time raising the main perspectives and issues that later will become central in our discussion.

To begin, let us review the historical materials that were presented in the first two chapters. Several centuries ago, prior to the industrial revolution, the large majority of people lived in small rural villages. The character and scale of the villages were based on an economy of mostly self-sufficient agriculture. Perhaps two hundred persons in size, the village encapsulated the lives of its residents: they were born, grew up, lived their daily lives, and died in the same village. The villagers lived in cottages and worked within walking distance of their homes; life was lived always in the close company of others. The village was an almost self-contained unit, a society in miniature, containing rich and poor, young and old, all living within visual distance of one another. For better and for worse, a small number of people shared a common life together within a limited space.

Many of these villages still exist in England, but their self-sufficiency and their common life are gone. Although they have an incontestable physical charm in an urban-industrial age, their traditional social, economic, and political fabric has been rent by outside forces. The village way of life was compromised much earlier in the United States and Sweden than in England due to the prominence of the independent farmstead. In each of the societies today the majority of people are housed in communities whose scale and character reflect a very different set of social and economic circumstances. With industrialization, it became necessary to bunch people together in larger aggregates so as to have available in one place both a mass of workers and a mass of consumers. As industries, and the linkages among industries, increased in scale, so did urban communities. These communities grew still larger due to population increases, and with mass transportation and the automobile they spread out over ever-larger areas.

None of the nations under consideration seriously attempted to curtail this dramatic shift of people and activities from small communities to large metropolitan areas (with a few modest exceptions, to be discussed in later chapters). They were not able to protect small villages, to divert people from metropolitan areas to smaller places, or to curtail metropolitan economic development. They rode with the forces of urban-industrial development, both unwilling and unable to counteract them. The result, if we are to believe public opinion polls, is a preponderance of people in each nation who are living in an alien environment. The residential preferences of most are smaller places. They are in metropolitan areas mainly for economic opportunity: jobs and higher incomes. If such opportunities were available in nonmetropolitan settings, they seemingly would move to those areas with alacrity, as indeed in recent years an increasing number have been able to do.[24]

This points up the inherent economic derivation of the metropolis: the metropolitan community is determined by the needs of the industrial economy much more than by the needs and desires of the residents. From an historical perspective this is neither surprising nor unusual. Save for those few urban places whose reason for being was religious worship, aristocratic display, or the achievement of a utopian idealism, most cities and towns of the past have been dictated by a crude economic determinism.[25] Yet economic determinism seems more pervasive than ever before: very few modern communities exist whose measure is not primarily economic. Compared to at least some of the communities of the past, the expression of noneconomic ideals in contemporary metropolitan settings seems all but snuffed out.

It is not only the massive scale but also much of the character of metropolitan areas that have been generated by economic forces. In each nation the focal point of the physical metropolis, and of life within the metropolis, is the shopping and business complex dedicated to the enhancement of buying and selling. At the central point of maximum metropolitan accessibility is a business district, with the tallest urban structures typically being commercial office buildings, especially banks. And in outlying areas the shopping center is the focal point of community life, whether it is reached by foot, by public transit, or by automobile.

Economic determinism cuts through the entire fabric of metropolitan ecology.[26] Although raw capitalism, that which stems from uncontrolled profit-seeking and the unrestricted use of private property, is mitigated more in Sweden than the United States, in the metropolitan areas of both nations the wealthy, for example, are able to buy up and hold onto the most desirable places to live. In Sweden it is the center city, steeped in charm and tradition; the new, raw housing in the mass-produced suburbs being left for persons of lesser means. In the United States the wealthy have commandeered the more desirable suburban areas, leaving for the poor the deteriorated districts that wealth long since has left behind.

A rival to economic determinism as a factor in metropolitan communities is the process of social differentiation, the division and specialization of social life. A major structural difference between the metropolitan areas of all three nations and the rural village, for example, is the extent to which people are residentially segregated in terms of income level. The difference may only seem reflective of the scale at which such segregation occurs. In the larger rural villages, rich and poor (except in the case of servants) tend to live apart from one another, perhaps in different sections of the community. And the nearest neighbor of each is likely to be of the same income level, thus forming small segregated neighborhoods. At the metropolitan scale, these small segregated neighborhoods become extensive single-class areas through sheer size alone.

This difference in geographic scale has a profound social consequence. In the rural village, the rich and poor still have daily face-to-face contact with one another; in the metropolis, they typically do not. To take the most serious extreme, the metropolitan poor may live in neighborhoods where, on a daily basis, they have contact only with others of equally low income. The effects of this geographic incestuousness have been pointed up in a myriad of studies on crime and delinquency, and multiproblem families. At the other extreme, the rich are cut off from the lives of the poor. Unlike in the village, the wealthy no longer have firsthand acquaintance with what it means to be poor; they have become geographically insulated from the lives of those less well off than themselves. And here television is no alternative to the full range of sense stimuli provided by face-to-face contact.

There is one aspect of metropolitan life in which economic affluence, together with transport technology, has permitted a strong departure from economic determinism. In the metropolitan areas of advanced societies, work and place of residence have been largely separated; people have been provided the means whereby they may distance themselves from employment centers, a situation that is especially desirable in the case of heavy industry.

In the rural villages and small towns of the past, workplace and residence place were, if not identical, at least in close proximity to one another. For centuries the family was a society's main production unit, and most work took place in the home, or in the fields connected to the home. Early industry often took the form of cottage industry, conducted by women and children in the home. Even when industry left the home environment, with the rise of the factory system, it remained very near a worker's place of residence; the absence of transport facilities required that workers' housing be within walking distance of workplaces. It was this circumstance, indeed, that caused some of the deplorable living conditions in the early industrial towns of Britain.

The separation of home and work has in turn led to two other fundamental metropolitan characteristics: the long journey to work and the dormitory area. Within some of the larger metropolitan areas in each nation, a person can spend up to two or more hours a day simply getting to work and back. This time is not subtracted from the normal workday; rather, it is subtracted from the time a person may spend at home. Save for the person who is able to read or do productive work on a long-haul commuter train, this time is frequently just lost from a person's life—it is put to no good use, either for work or leisure. Yet with the decreasing length of the workday over the years, this loss of time is not usually regarded as very serious. Within maximum limits, for example, the length of the journey to work is not often a compelling factor in the selection of a place to live.

It is the creation of metropolitan dormitory areas that is more socially consequential. While such areas are cut off from work, they tend also to be cut off from community life. Especially for those who must inhabit these areas during the day, and there are many such persons—children, housewives, the unemployed, the sick, the elderly—these areas are often felt to be lifeless. Perhaps this is a small price to pay for the peace, quiet, and relative safety that dormitory areas also engender, but I will suggest that the problem is more serious than most people realize.

The dormitory area is but one instance of the way in which, in the metropolitan areas of advanced societies, the pieces that once made up the small, self-contained community have become geographically and socially differentiated in an extreme form. Especially in the United States, shopping as well as jobs have been removed from residential areas and given a place of their own. Cultural pursuits and recreation take place in still other geographic locales. When to these community functions is added the immense residential segregation of people, discussed above, it becomes clear that social differentiation must be accorded at least the same importance as economic determinism as a factor that dominates the metropolitan fabric.

The process of social differentiation is further expressed in the situation of the metropolitan household. It is incorrect to say that the typical preindustrial and rural household consisted of an extended family, for often housing was physically too small for such a large group. But grandparents and other relatives at least lived very nearby. And the boundary between household and community was a very permeable one; many different people passed into and out of the household on a regular basis.

In metropolitan areas today, the household is a strongly differentiated locale consisting of the nuclear family, or even just one or two unrelated individuals, clearly separated and apart from the surrounding environment. Relatives tend to live at some distance, perhaps out of the metropolitan area entirely. The boundary of the household is relatively rigid; entry is gained only after a knock on the door or a ring of the bell; in many cases, a telephone call in advance is required. The privatized household containing a small number of individuals is as typical of the Swedish apartment as it is of the American detached house and the British row house.

Thus emerges a common picture of metropolitan communities in these three societies that is one of a residential environment, too large and in many ways alien from the residents' perspective, that is shaped mainly by economic and material interests. Within this environment, many of the main dimensions and phases of society have become segregated and geographically scattered, leaving people separated from one another and residential neighborhoods cut off from community life. The private household, with its handful of inhabitants, still further insulates the individual from the world outside. Held together largely by the products of advanced technology in communication and transportation, the metropolitan community may be well adapted to the pursuit by many of private pleasure. But at the same time it presents, I shall argue, what may best be described as a public plight.

## Notes

1. An excellent review of these early efforts of municipal reform may be found in William Ashworth, *The Genesis of Modern British Town Planning* (London: Routledge & Kegan Paul, 1954), parts 1 and 2.
2. See Peter Hall, *Urban and Regional Planning* (London: Penguin, 1975), pp. 30ff. Also see Asa Briggs, *Victorian Cities* (London: Odhams Books, 1963); and H.J. Dyos, *Victorian Suburb* (Leicester: Leicester University Press, 1966).
3. Vast slum areas continued to exist in the larger English cities well into this century. See, for example, Albert Fried and Richard Elman, eds., *Charles Booth's London* (Baltimore: Penguin Books, 1968); and Robert Roberts, *The Classic Slum* (Baltimore: Penguin Books, 1971).
4. This is generally the form, for example, of Chicago in the 1920s that was the subject of so much research by the Chicago school of American sociology. See Robert E. Park and E.W. Burgess, *The City* (Chicago: University of Chicago Press, 1925, 1967); and Ernest W. Burgess, and D.J. Bogue, eds., *Urban Sociology* (Chicago: University of Chicago Press, 1964).
5. Lennart Jörberg, "Structural Change and Economic Growth in Nineteenth Century Sweden," in S. Koblick, ed., *Sweden's Development from Poverty to Affluence* (Minneapolis: University of Minnesota Press), p. 93.
6. Bengt O.H. Johansson, "From Agrarian to Industrial State," in *New Towns and Old*, ed. Hans Erland Heineman (Stockholm: Swedish Institute, 1975), pp. 22-52.
7. *The Biography of a People* (Stockholm: Royal Ministry of Foreign Affairs, 1974), pp. 75-77; and Kurt Samuelsson, *From Great Power to Welfare State* (London: Allen & Unwin, 1968), pp. 161-63.
8. Ella Ödmann and Gun-Britt Dahlberg, *Urbanization in Sweden* (Stockholm: Allmänna Förlaget, 1970), pp. 36-39.
9. See Franklin D. Scott, *Sweden: The Nation's History* (Minneapolis: University of Minnesota Press, 1977), ch.16; and Jörberg, "Structural Change and Economic Growth."
10. The best discussions of the Swedish welfare state, in my opinion, are Marquis W. Childs, *Sweden: The Middle Way* (New Haven: Yale University Press, 1936), for the very early years, and Richard F. Tomasson, *Sweden: Prototype of Modern Society* (New York: Random House, 1970), for the two decades following World War II.
11. See Richard Scase, *Social Democracy in Capitalist Society* (London: Croom Helm, 1977); and Francis G. Castles, *The Social Democratic Image of Society* (London: Routledge & Kegan Paul, 1978).
12. Samuelsson, *From Great Power to Welfare State*, pp. 148-50.
13. For a good recent discussion, see Thomas Bender, *Community and Social Change in America* (New Brunswick, NJ: Rutgers University Press, 1978).
14. Michael Zukerman, *Peaceable Kingdoms: New England Towns in the Eighteenth Century* (New York: Norton, 1978), p.4.
15. See Lewis Mumford, *The City in History* (New York: Harcourt, Brace & World, 1961), pp. 330-33.
16. A fine review of life in such towns is Lewis Atherton, *Main Street on the Middle Border* (Bloomington: Indiana University Press, 1954). See also Page Smith, *As a City upon a Hill: The Town in American History* (Cambridge: MIT Press,

1973); and John Reps, *The Making of Urban America* (Princeton: Princeton University Press, 1965).

17. Anthony F.C. Wallace, *Rockdale* (New York: Norton, 1972), pp. 4-5.

18. See Carl Bode, ed., *American Life in the 1840's* (Garden City, NY: Doubleday/ Anchor, 1967).

19. For an interesting account of conditions in Philadelphia in 1830-60, which may be compared with nearby Rockdale, see Sam Bass Warner, Jr., *The Private City* (Philadelphia: University of Pennsylvania Press, 1968), chs. 3-7.

20. Quoted in Howard P. Chudacoff, *The Evolution of American Urban Society* (Englewood Cliffs, NJ: Prentice-Hall, 1975) p. 44.

21. Quoted in: Morton White and Lucia White, *The Intellectual versus the City* (New York: Mentor Books, 1964), p. 35.

22. Ibid.

23. Adna Weber, *The Growth of Cities in the Nineteenth Century* (Ithaca, NY: Cornell University Press, 1963; originally published, 1899); and Blake McKelvey, *The Emergence of Metropolitan America* (New Brunswick, NJ: Rutgers University Press, 1968).

24. In a 1975 survey of many nations around the world, the Americans and West Europeans gave similar answers to the question: "If you could live anywhere you wish which of the following would you prefer?" The North American responses were: large city, 13 percent; small city, 29 percent; town or village, 21 percent; and rural area, 37 percent. The European responses were: large city, 19 percent; small city, 22 percent; town or village, 27 percent; and rural area, 32 percent. Survey Research Consultants, *Index to International Public Opinion: 1978-79* (Westport, Conn.: Greenwood Press, 1980).

25. See Max Weber, *The City* (1921); and Henri Pirenne, *Medieval Cities* (Garden City, NY: Doubleday/Anchor, 1925).

26. William K. Tabb and L. Sawers, eds., *Marxism and the Metropolis* (NY: Oxford University Press, 1978); and C.G. Pickvance, ed., *Urban Sociology* (London: Tavistock, 1976).

# PART II

# FORM

# 3

# The Metropolitan Setting: A Portrait of Three Metropolitan Areas

An obvious place to begin our examination of metropolitan life in the three societies is the metropolitan setting—the visible, tangible dimension of the metropolis with which an outsider first comes into contact. The setting, or what urban designers refer to as form, typically refers to the built environment of a community: all the houses and other buildings and uses of the land, including modes of transportation, and the arrangements and interconnections of those uses in space. In sociological usage, the concept of setting or form is often expanded to include the arrangement of people in space, people differentiated according to such social characteristics as age, sex, ethnicity, and social status.[1] This expanded concept is the one used in the following pages.

In giving first consideration to metropolitan form we do not mean to imply that form is necessarily a prime determinant of social life, in the sense that "function follows form." The reverse position probably would be the more accurate: "form follows function." But as Winston Churchill once said, "We shape our buildings, and afterwards our buildings shape us," and his remark doubtless applies as much to the residential environment as to individual buildings.[2] The relationship between human societies and their environmental backdrop is surely two-way. It is not the intent of this book, however, carefully to develop the environment-behavior interrelationship.[3] Let us be content with the neutral position: metropolitan form is the container within which metropolitan life takes place. And as such, it provides a tangible handle with which to begin to unlock the complexities of that life.

To provide raw materials for the ensuing chapters, it seems useful to start with a comparative description of the "typical" metropolitan setting in each nation. A description of the metropolitan setting in one's own society may seem an overly obvious exercise; it is, of course, intended more for the foreign reader. But there is also certainly the chance that new insights into one's own setting may be gleaned by viewing it, as is done here, as if through the eyes of a foreign observer.

What is a typical metropolitan setting? Because so many variables are involved, any example that is put forth can always be subject to question. For the following discussion I have selected three metropolitan areas of about the same number of inhabitants that seem reasonably to represent each nation.

## Stockholm and Seattle

The United States and Sweden are similar in so many respects—per capita national income, a strong orientation to economic progress, and relatively abundant land—that it is surprising to find such striking differences in the character of their metropolitan areas. Partly this is due to the scale of population: there is nothing in Sweden approaching the scale of a New York, Chicago, or Los Angeles. Partly it is due to population makeup: the United States is a nation of immigrants; Sweden's population is mostly homogeneous. Thus a comparison of massive, polyglot New York City with relatively diminutive and socially undiversified Stockholm would yield many obvious and not too enlightening results. But suppose Stockholm were compared with a U.S. city of similar size and population character? The example I have chosen is Seattle.

Both the Stockholm and Seattle metropolitan areas have approximately the same population, close to a million and a half people.[4] And Seattle, unlike many American cities, has a very small minority population. Indeed, Seattle has a relatively large population of Americans of Scandinavian descent. But there are other notable similarities as well. Both are "water cities," having a sea access and abundant lakes and rivers; boating and water sports are therefore common pastimes of the two populations. Also, Seattle is quite comparable to Stockholm in that it is a relatively isolated and self-contained agglomeration of people. It is not, like many eastern cities, one part of a great sprawling megalopolis that may extend for hundreds of miles. Like Stockholm, when Seattle ends the countryside begins.

Yet Seattle does not end as soon or as abruptly as Stockholm. With the same population as Stockholm, Seattle uses twice the land area, and when viewed from the air, appears to be twice as large. Its metropolitan boundary is by no means clear-cut. Approached by air, Seattle signals its presence well in advance: scattered houses, shops, and gas stations begin to thicken. They soon appear as fingerlike projections, commanding both sides of the roadways entering the city. One is never quite sure at what point the rural countryside ends and the physical metropolis of Seattle actually begins.

Approaching Stockholm by air is a very different matter; one gets little advance warning of the metropolis. Suddenly pristine countryside gives way to a high-density built environment. Stockholm has very little rural-urban fringe: the use of land is either rural or urban, not a mixture of the two. Visually, this yields a strong sense of order, and signals a clear ideological separation of town and country as two very distinct worlds.

In Seattle, the visual appearance is one of ambiguity. It is as if its citizens are struggling to get out of town but not quite succeeding. They end up still under the pull of the city, surrounded by a quasi-rural environment intermixed with desultory urban forms. If Stockholm's urban growth is strongly by design, Seattle's appears almost as if by chance.

The qualitative assessment of these air views is of course quite relative. To most Americans Seattle is one of the most beautiful cities in the nation. On a clear summer day, with the water shimmering against the rich green forests, myriad white boats moving to and fro, and the snow-capped Cascades and Mt. Rainier as a backdrop, there are few lovelier urban scenes. Perhaps it is only the eye of the social scientist or planner that would capture the sharp contrasts between the two cities, but I think that any perceptive air traveler to both cities could also not fail to note them.

Most Americans would pay scant attention to another dominant visual feature of the Seattle landscape that sets it apart from Stockholm: the ever-present automobile. Does a fish notice the water around it? The American car, very large by world standards, may often be an attractive object in isolation, but in profusion it cannot be judged an aesthetically pleasing element by anyone's standard. Compared to Stockholm, Seattle appears to swim in a sea of cars and car appurtenances, such as roadways, parking lots, and gas stations.

It is not just that Seattle cars are larger than Stockholm autos. There are twice as many of them, and they are relied on much more heavily. Seattle does have a bus system, but the average household owns two cars and the great majority of Seattle working residents use the automobile to get to work. In Stockholm, only 7 percent of households have two cars, while 45 percent own no automobile at all. The relatively low Swedish ownership is not because Swedes cannot afford cars (although taxes make cars much more expensive than in the United States), it is because they do not need cars. Sixty percent of all Stockholm journeys to work are made by public transportation, and another 20 percent on foot.[5]

The omnipresence of the automobile in Seattle occurs for another reason: the relatively low density of Seattle surroundings make it stand out. Streets are wide and houses are low, parking lots are often enormous and typically are in open air at ground level. And freeways are often elevated, giving the car that right of way with the fewest impediments. Unlike in Sweden, the automobile is not masked by high buildings, enclosed parking decks, underground passageways, and pedestrian-only areas. It is exposed for all to see.

The reason there are so many automobiles in Seattle is that so many of her citizens want to own and use them. But the reason they want to own or use them is in part because they have to. Seventy percent of occupied residential structures in Seattle are detached, single-family houses on small (or sometimes very large) parcels of privately owned land. It is the automobile that makes such low-density living possible. At the residential densities generated by detached, single-family houses, public transportation becomes inefficient, and the automobile is made a necessity.

Let us make a brief digression to consider the economics of personal transportation. If mass transit is designed with enough collection points that these all can be reached by people on foot, the system becomes too expensive and much too slow. On the other hand, if collection points can be reached only by private vehicle, the system deteriorates because people would typically much rather stay in the required automobile to their destination than change modes of transportation. The circle sets in: The more people own and rely on private automobiles, the more the public transportation system deteriorates from lack of use, and the more the system deteriorates, the more people will buy and use automobiles. Once a car is bought, it is cheaper (for Americans) to use it than to pay both for public transportation and for the car's depreciation while parked in the garage.

The automobile is also a very seductive device. Compared to walking, riding requires the expenditure of much less energy and time and is therefore more comfortable and efficient. Americans come to use the automobile even for very short distances, such as trips to the corner store or to a friend down the street, while people in most other nations are much more likely to walk short distances.

Stockholm's planners have been well aware of the seductive nature of the automobile, and of its corrosive effects on public transportation. They have even gone so far, in some areas, as deliberately to locate car owners' private parking places farther from their residences than the nearest public transportation stop. Thus some of the comfort has been taken out of private automobile use. At the same time, the public transportation system is often as comfortable and efficient as the private automobile because it is fast, clean, reliable, and (due to heavy public subsidization) relatively low-cost. Seattle has only a struggling bus system, but Stockholm has an elaborate subway system (built since World War II) supplemented by extensive feeder bus lines.

The excellence of Stockholm's public transportation has not been gained by public subsidization alone. More important is the fact that the city largely has been designed to serve the transportation system.[6] Instead of living in dispersed single-family houses, Stockholm residents (76 percent) live in apartment buildings (typically three or four stories) that are grouped around public transport collection points. Thus many Stockholm residents, if they cannot walk to work, can at least comfortably walk to public transportation.

It should not be thought that, in relation to urban form, transportation is the tail that wags the dog. Other factors, such as economic and political pressures and the demand for housing, are of at least equal importance in accounting for the character of Stockholm today. The full range of factors is discussed in the next chapter. But just as Seattle would be impossible without the heavy use of private automobiles, Stockholm would be a vastly different place were it not for its public transport system.

No matter how much time Americans may spend in their cars, it nevertheless is their homes that matter most. The differences between the typical dwelling units in Seattle and Stockholm are perhaps the most significant of all differences from the residents' point of view. The American lives with more private dwelling space by far than do people in any other part of the world. The typical Seattle house has five relatively large rooms, a private garage for one or more cars, and a private yard; all are usually owned rather than rented. The typical Stockholm dwelling has three or four rooms, a parking space separate from the dwelling, and no private land. Rental is the most usual form of housing tenure in Stockholm. And while the Seattle resident's dwelling space is relatively well insulated from the neighbor's by two walls and twenty or thirty feet of open space, the Stockholm dwelling space abuts the neighbor's, separated only by a party wall.

The amount of private dwelling space a person has is a measure of his or her level of consumption of consumer goods, if for no other reason than that such goods must be put somewhere. Although Sweden has the highest consumption of consumer goods in Europe, for reasons to be discussed in later chapters, the level of consumer spending falls somewhat behind that in the United States. The dwelling of the Seattle resident, in comparison to the Swede's, is more likely to contain two television sets, a dishwasher, a clothes dryer, and such large sports equipment as a ping-pong or pool table. In this sense, the American dwelling unit is not only larger but more self-contained.

Yet a number of other factors make the dwelling-unit situation in the two cities less discrepant than it first appears. There are fewer people in the Stockholm household than in the Seattle (2.0 versus 2.5); more Stockholm women work (over 65 percent versus about 50 percent for Seattle); and many more children are in public day care centers, meaning that there are fewer household members using the dwelling unit during the day. Moreover, facilities for washing and drying clothes are often provided within the apartment building for residents there, and sometimes sports facilities are also available.

The advantages of the American's private space are also offset to some extent in Sweden by the public provision of facilities close to the home. The American's dwelling unit is more self-contained than the Swede's, but the opposite holds true for the local neighborhood, which in Stockholm is more likely to contain nurseries and day care centers, parks and playgrounds for all ages, walking trails and sitting areas, and publicly maintained gardens. So the significant difference between the two cities in regard to facilities used on a daily basis is to be found not so much in their presence or availability as in their distribution and location.

Just as automobiles and single-family detached houses signal dispersed urban development at low densities, so public transportation and apartment buildings suggest concentrated, high-density development. One would expect to find less open space, land that is not built upon, in the higher-density environment. Surely this is what one does find in the dense cities of Eastern Europe, or even the eastern United States. It is a bit of a surprise, then, to discover that Stockholm, with half of Seattle's land area, has probably every bit as much open space. And far more of Stockholm's open space is truly open to the public.

Some cities build at high densities to crowd people onto the land, but Stockholm's residential densities are, as much as anything, for the purpose of preserving a great amount of open space for public use and visual appearance. Despite its multifamily housing, Stockholm appears to be a much less congested city than Seattle. Fingers of green, untouched by human buildings, extend all the way from the countryside to the city's interior. Indeed, many of Stockholm's better apartment developments have aspects that are more country than city; the settings are parklike, not busy city streets.

Seattle also has many public parks, but they are apart from residential areas. One does not live in them, or with them; occasionally one drives to them for a few hours of use. The American alternative is to give each household a small park of its own: the private yard. Most of Seattle's "open space" is in the form of yards around houses—small, fenced, and private.

The combination of conditions discussed above gives rise to another very distinctive difference between the two cities: Seattle is much less oriented to the pedestrian. Because the car is ever available, walking has nearly assumed the character of a vestigial activity. If one does chance to walk, it is difficult to avoid the (often physically dangerous) domination of the automobile and the pervasiveness of private property. One typically must be prepared to share public space with the automobile on grossly unequal terms.

In Stockholm, not only must residents walk more of necessity but the environment tends to invite the activity. Automobiles are less dominant and far more segregated from the domain of pedestrians. Indeed, there are many public places where the world of the automobile can be left entirely behind, whereas in the United States such a circumstance can typically be found only in enclosed mall shopping centers on a city's periphery, and in some cases in a limited central city zone. As much as anything else, private, fenced-in yards lend plausibility to the view that Americans' homes are their castles. But the protectionist instinct of Americans extends well beyond the private home and yard to the neighborhood beyond. The neighborhoods of Americans tend to be more homogeneous in terms of social class, and often also in terms of race and ethnicity, than do neighborhoods in other advanced nations.

People throughout history have residentially segregated themselves to some extent in terms of occupational and income levels, but at the scale of rural villages, the size of such segregated neighborhoods is very small. At the scale of an American metropolis, the segregation of neighborhoods by class assumes massive proportions. Vast areas of Seattle housing are nothing but working class, or upper middle class. The social classes are thus physically out of contact with one another. In the growing-up process, young people of different social classes are physically isolated from one another in the early years and remain so perhaps until reaching a consolidated high school, the sending area of which spans several class-bound areas, or even until going off to college or university.

Stockholm has many class-bound neighborhoods, especially in the early suburbs constructed around the turn of the century and in the most recently built suburbs that house many immigrant groups. But the chances are much greater in Stockholm than in Seattle of finding neighborhoods that are class mixed, with children of different classes attending the same schools, using the same parks, and sharing the same turf.

One type of class-segregated neighborhood commonly found in American cities is entirely absent in Stockholm: the slum. Sweden does not have the large "underclass" that makes up slum populations the world over, and Stockholm's poorest tend to be scattered around in many different neighborhoods, in line with the diminished class segregation just noted. Compared to most other American cities, Seattle has a relatively small underclass population, and its slums are much less noxious and extensive than are those of the older industrial metropolises. Yet the characteristic American pattern of central business district surrounded by sections of slum-like housing is nonetheless quite evident. Indeed, the term *skid row* originated in Seattle; it means an area where people are on the *skids*, a term derived from the lumber industry.

Stockholm's lack of inner-city slum areas is symptomatic of an even more radical dissimilarity between the two cities concerning the spatial arrangement of residents. The residents of many Stockholm suburbs are of a lower occupational and income status than are residents of the inner city. As one goes further from the center of the city, the class level of the residents tends to drop. This is precisely the reverse of the American pattern, where the suburbs are associated with the wealthier classes and the inner cities with the poor, and the farther from downtown one lives, the wealthier one is likely to be. Hints of the Stockholm pattern can be seen in the older cities of the U.S. East, where bastions of upper- and upper-middle-class households still cling to small sections of the inner city—Park Avenue in New York and Rittenhouse Square in Philadelphia are examples. But there are few such hints in Seattle. The inner city houses the lower classes, and the wealthy live on the outskirts. The middle class lies in between.

In its pattern of residential differentiation, Stockholm perpetuates the form of preindustrial cities. For reasons of defense, and to be near jobs, shops, and city services in an age when most transport was by foot, the wealthy of preindustrial cities commanded the city centers, leaving the poor to make do as best they could on the periphery. Often the poor were forced entirely outside the city wall. Seattle still has a city center but the remainder of the preindustrial city scheme is not to be seen; because it is a twentieth-century city, this is much to be expected. But, paradoxically, most of present-day Stockholm was also built in the twentieth century.

The characteristic pattern of residential differentiation has important implications for the character of each metropolitan area's central district. Downtown Seattle is mainly a daytime center for business and, to a lesser extent, for shopping, and has few permanent nighttime residents. Because persons with the most buying power and the most enthusiasm for "culture" live far from the center, shopping and some cultural facilities have tended to follow the suburban trend. Like many other downtowns, downtown Seattle has made and is making major efforts to revive itself, but with only partial success. Unless they happen to work in Seattle, many suburban residents seldom if ever go to town, contenting themselves instead with the large shopping centers on the metropolitan area's periphery, many of which try to provide some of the cultural and environmental amenities of the classic "downtown."

Stockholm, in contrast, is still what was once commonly referred to as a cosmopolitan city. It may lack the variety and the vitality of such continental cities as Paris, Amsterdam, and Munich but, like them, has a large, inner-city nighttime population of the wealthiest classes, who support the theater, fine restaurants, and expensive shops. What it lacks in vitality (the result of such factors as size, national character, and even climate) it makes up for in those environmental qualities that enhance its livability for the average middle-class or upper-middle-class family. Especially for a large city, it has strikingly high standards in cleanliness, safety, quiet, transportation efficiency, and availability of such services as parks and schools, qualities not commonly associated with city living, especially in the United States. It is due to these qualities, of course, that so many higher-class families remain in the inner city, where they may pursue a graciously urbane life-style that has all but vanished in the United States.

Stockholm, too, has outlying suburban shopping centers, but they have not siphoned off center-city activity to the same degree as those in Seattle. And the character of downtown Stockholm, together with the ease of transportation access, make it a far more important magnet for all of the city's residents than is the case in the American city.

Let us summarize the points we have been making. Despite many similarities between the two nations, especially an equivalent per capita national income, the United States and Sweden have evolved two strikingly dissimilar patterns of urban or metropolitan form. This emerges clearly in a comparison of Seattle and Stockholm, two metropolitan areas that have the basic similarities of population size, geographic setting, and population makeup. The principal urban patterns of these two places stand in many respects at opposite ends of a continuum. Seattle is dispersed, even scattered, with a comparatively weak downtown area and a population that lives for the most part in detached, single-family houses. The area is held together, one could also say dominated, by the automobile. Stockholm is denser and geographically more compact, and contains a more dominant central city. Its residents live in apartments in medium-rise, multifamily structures. Without private land, they depend more heavily on pedestrian-oriented public spaces. And the area is held together by a mass transit system.

Although neither Seattle nor Stockholm is typical in every respect of other metropolitan areas in their respective nations, the elements of urban form that they manifest are very characteristic. Two-thirds of all Americans live in metropolitan areas with center cities of at least 50,000 in population, some 284 areas in all. Most of these are smaller than Seattle; 21 are larger. Urban areas in the East, built at an earlier stage of history, have some characteristics more like Stockholm's. They are denser, with more persons living in apartments; the downtown areas play a more dominant role, as does mass transportation. But the newer urban areas in the South and Southwest tend to be even further along the continuum than Seattle, with lower densities and more scatteration, weaker downtown areas, and greater reliance on the automobile. All metropolitan areas in the United States, large and small, are much more like one another than they are like comparable areas in Sweden, with their single-family homes and automobiles, their declining central areas, and their class-segregated neighborhoods, which increase in income level the further they are from the city center. Indeed, the newer suburban areas across the nation tend to be almost identical in structure and appearance, with the exception of larger lot sizes in the East than in the Far West, plus obvious climatic and geographic differences.

One should also note that Seattle is generally regarded as a better place to live than most other metropolitan areas in the United States. It scores at or near the top of cities in desirability as measured by public opinion polls, but also by such indicators as crime rates, climate and air quality, level of public service, percentage of poor housing and welfare cases, and proximity to recreational areas.[7]

Stockholm is the capital as well as the largest city in Sweden. The next-largest metropolitan area in Sweden, Gothenburg (Göteborg), is less than half Stockholm's size, and only six urban areas in Sweden are over 100,000 population. Considerably less than half the population live in these six areas, so although Sweden is fully as urbanized as the United States, and perhaps a little more so (depending upon the criteria used), the urban population tends to be located in smaller places.

Like its counterparts in other nations, Stockholm as a capital city has a great deal going for it—a special concentration of culture, shopping, jobs, and governmental facilities. And income levels in Stockholm are slightly higher than in the rest of the country, but this is offset by a higher cost of living. Yet apart from Stockholm's size and density, special downtown assets and subway systems, her urban form is very characteristic of most urban places in Sweden. The continuing viability of downtown as a residential environment, apartment living, good public transportation, the clean separation of rural and urban, and the class integration of neighborhoods, all typify much of contemporary Swedish urban life.

### Enter England: The Case of Birmingham

If the metropolitan forms characteristic of the United States and Sweden can be conceived as two poles of a continuum, the form of British metropolitan areas falls close to the middle of that continuum. This may not be surprising, for although Britain is distinctively "European" in contrast with the United States, the British do not think of themselves as European, and in many respects Britain is the most American of the European nations. The cultural similarities—not the least of which is a common language—

are perhaps best viewed as a legacy of the former British colonial status of the United States. Also prominent is a strong individualism in both nations nurtured by many centuries without foreign domination. In marked contrast to the United States, however, Britain has high population density (because of a small land area), relative population homogeneity, and British history (and sense of history), all to be developed in the next chapter.

Birmingham is Britain's second-largest city. Its roughly 1 million people place it in the same size class as Seattle and Stockholm (Britain's largest city, London, is much larger, with over 6 million). Birmingham is much older than Seattle, with a period of intense industrialization that was well before Stockholm's. And its economic base today is more heavily industrial than those of the other two cities. While perhaps not providing an ideal comparison, it nevertheless has the characteristics of urban form that are very typical of the British metropolitan scene.

The predominant Birmingham dwelling unit is the terrace (row) house. The upwardly mobile family aspires to a semidetached house. After World War II a substantial number of high- and medium-rise multifamily structures were built, but the terrace house appears in low rows on street after street, giving the city the appearance of large areas of Philadelphia or Baltimore. Most of the houses built during the late Victorian era and in the early years of the twentieth century have a monotonous uniformity, which does not win them any aesthetic awards. Yet with their lace curtains and often well-kept doorways, they have a certain coziness, a timeless, comfortable quality that comes from their being an expression of a long tradition of urban life.

The older terrace houses almost completely fill up the residential landscape, giving Birmingham the appearance, by U.S. and Swedish standards, of significant congestion. This appearance is accentuated by narrow streets, laid out long before the automobile arrived. Although British auto ownership is today only half that of the United States, and behind that of Sweden, the auto has nonetheless become an ever-present and obtrusive part of the Birmingham street scene. Few of the terrace houses have garages, so the cars are parked on both sides of the narrow streets in unbroken lines. In many areas the small front yard has been paved over and turned into an open-air carport. Thus the automobile is often an even more obtrusive part of the urban landscape than it is in the United States.

In the available amount of private dwelling space, the Birmingham resident ranks ahead of the Swede but behind the American. The private space of the British resident is even more extensive compared to the Swede when the rear yard is added, as it must be. Almost always fenced in, the rear yard is a true projection of the living area of the house, typically with space for sitting, for gardening, for hanging the wash, and for some outdoor storage.

The Birmingham landscape presents many more contrasts than are found in Seattle or Stockholm. There are large areas of terrace housing in slum condition, often made worse because, with redevelopment in the offing, it is undermaintained. Massive areas have already been redeveloped, to a form and appearance that are quite distinctive from the land uses that preceded them. The redeveloped areas have been substantially de-congested, given a large amount of open green space, are traversed by curved instead of straight streets, and the areas rebuilt after World War II are devoted to high-rise buildings. Thus Birmingham has a pockmarked quality: older, congested areas of terrace housing are interspersed with redeveloped areas of medium- and high-rise buildings in a parklike setting.

The high-rise housing is an anachronism on the Birmingham landscape. Built for reasons of both expediency and architectural ideology during the postwar housing shortage, it is not desired by most Birmingham residents and socially has been less than successful in many areas. Yet the strong proclivity of the British people for ground-level housing, a cultural trait for which Britons are well known among Europeans, has again prevailed and current rehousing programs have returned to the terrace house, albeit in a modernized package.

In view of its building density, standing between that of Stockholm and Seattle, it is not surprising that Birmingham is on the borderline of effi-ciency in mass transit. The city is served principally by buses, with a system much more extensive than that of Seattle. Bus service is supplemented by an aging commuter rail service, especially important for some outlying suburban areas. But compared to Stockholm, many more residents get to work by automobile.

The essential role of the automobile is attested to by the appearance of Birmingham's heavily redeveloped central business district. Even more than in Seattle, the district is dominated by automobile appurtenances, especially an elevated road circumnavigating the downtown and never far from view, and an abundance of ramps leading to multideck parking garages. The intent of these structures, and the planners have not been unsuccessful at this, is to entirely clear automobiles from the downtown core. In internal appearance resembling a large, enclosed suburban shop-ping mall in the United States, center-city Birmingham has become a pedestrian only, multistory shopping complex.

Intensive redevelopment, together with the lack of major shopping facili-ties in outlying areas, has facilitated greatly the daily flow of shoppers to center-city Birmingham. In this respect it is quite unlike American cities, where shopping has been pulled from the central city. But the redevelop-ment has done little to encourage the use of downtown Birmingham as a nighttime, residential district. Birmingham is more American than Swedish in this respect: it does not contain a large center-city population of urban and cosmopolitan households. By and large central Birmingham is only a commercial district surrounded by extensive areas of housing for lower-income groups. From center to periphery, the quality of housing and the income level of the population increases, with the wealthiest households tending to live on the city's outskirts.

There are two strong exceptions to this American-type urban pattern. British neighborhoods tend to be slightly more class mixed than those of American cities. In Birmingham, within a small neighborhood, households are likely to be of varying class levels. And the tendency toward higher income levels as distance from the center city increases has been compromised by the construction, on Birmingham's outermost flanks, of housing estates for workers. In this respect the Swedish pattern is duplicated, the more so because many of these working-class housing estates contain mostly high-rise multifamily buildings. Thus, the building densities at the outskirts are sometimes higher than those closer to the city's center.

It is all the more surprising, then, to discover that the Birmingham metropolitan area comes to an abrupt end. Despite its placement in the extensively urbanized area known as the West-Midlands conurbation (population 2.3 million), urban sprawl around Birmingham has been drastically curtailed. Beyond the high-rise housing is pure countryside, still in use for agricultural purposes.

In summary, Birmingham is in numerous aspects of metropolitan form a compromise between the extreme high- and low-density settings of Stockholm and Seattle. It is relatively compact, with the most common house type being the terrace house, with small private yard, but mixed with other housing types of both higher and lower density. Urban sprawl is minimized, yet the downtown area, although holding a more dominant commercial position than the Seattle downtown, lacks the overall vitality and prominence of the Swedish central city. Birmingham residents rely more heavily on the automobile than Stockholm residents, but are able to depend upon a mass transit system superior to that of Seattle. Neighborhood development shows some of the features of the American city, especially the presence of both inner-city slums and wealthy outlying suburbs, but in the neighborhood intermixing of social classes and in outlying working class housing estates the Swedish pattern is suggested.

The characteristics of Birmingham are to a very large degree traits of other British metropolitan areas. Inner-city London is much more fully developed as a residential area for the upper and upper-middle classes, and outer London has been more subject to urban sprawl. The New Towns of Britain contrast by virtue of their newness, although they represent only a very small part of the urban population. And in Britain's very old towns, of which there are many, a medieval street pattern with some remaining medieval buildings greatly complicates but also adds charm and diversity to the downtown areas, giving them a quality of deep tradition and rootedness. But each of these city types is at the same time a bastion of the terrace house in neighborhoods congested by narrow streets overstocked with cars, the small, private rear yard, the local specialty shops and the still commercially vibrant downtown.

Thus we have a sketch of three metropolitan areas of similar size in countries of similar wealth and culture in which are found surprising differences of urban form. How are we to account for these differences? That is the subject of the following chapter.

## Notes

1. D.I. Scargill, *The Form of Cities* (London: Bell & Hyman, 1979); and Werner Z. Hirsch, *Urban Life and Form* (New York: Holt, Rinehart & Winston, 1963).
2. Quoted in Robert K. Merton, "The Social Psychology of Housing," in *Current Trends in Social Psychology*, ed. Wayne Dennis (Pittsburgh: University of Pittsburgh Press, 1948), p. 204.
3. Excellent reviews of the environment-behavior relationship in urban settings can be found in W. Michelson, *Man and His Urban Environment* (Reading, MA: Addison-Wesley, 1976); J. Douglas Porteous, *Environment and Behavior* (Reading, MA: Addison-Wesley, 1977); and Irwin Altman and Martin M. Chemers, *Culture and Environment* (Belmont, Calif.: Wadsworth, 1980).
4. In the 1980 Census, the Seattle-Everett metropolitan area was the twenty-second largest in the United States, with a population of 1,600,944; the Stockholm area is the largest in Sweden, with a 1980 population of about 1,400,000.
5. Data sources: U.S. and Swedish censuses of population and housing.
6. See David Popenoe, *The Suburban Environment: Sweden and the U.S.* (Chicago: University of Chicago Press, 1977), ch. 2: and Thomas J. Anton, *Governing Greater Stockholm* (Berkeley: University of California Press, 1975), ch. 4.
7. The Seattle-Everett metropolitan area was ranked fifth among 277 metropolitan areas as a good place to live by Richard Boyer and David Savageau, *Places Rated Almanac* (New York: Rand McNally, 1981).

# 4

# Explaining the Dissimilarities
# of Metropolitan Form

In this chapter the characteristic metropolitan environments of three advanced societies, the United States, Great Britain, and Sweden, are analyzed from a comparative sociocultural and historical perspective, focusing on the reasons for their dissimilarities. A full explanation of the causes of urban form is well beyond the scope of this inquiry. Moreover, the theory of urban form, and relatively complete analysis of urban form in each nation, are available elsewhere in the literature.[1] Here we shall seek to bring to the analysis of urban form a cross-societal perspective. Too often, in studies looking at a single society, technological and economic factors emerge as the major determinants of urban form. The main factors emphasized are the automobile, the working of the real estate market, and the capitalist domination of the economic system, the latter figuring very prominently in recent neo-Marxian interpretations of urban form.[2] Yet as will be developed here, these factors assume quite different proportions when placed against their larger cultural and historical backdrop.

Despite common capitalist characteristics, the three nations discussed here are strikingly unalike in the way in which urban-industrial development has been physically expressed, as was described in the last chapter. While each nation is highly metropolitan in character, with a large majority of residents residing in metropolitan areas, Sweden and the United States manifest opposite extremes of metropolitan or urban form. Sweden's urban areas are highly compact, with most residents living in small apartments and relying on mass transportation and other public services. In contrast, most urban areas in the United States are extremely dispersed, with the majority of residents living in detached single-family houses and relying on private automobiles along with a variety of other private services.

But the differences do not stop there: Swedish urban areas are contained,

with a definite boundary separating them from protected rural countryside, while American cities sprawl into their rural environs. In Swedish
cities the downtown areas have been well maintained, enabling them to
continue dominating the metropolitan area; American central cities have
been dying a lingering death. Finally, the social classes are comparatively
intermixed in Swedish urban residential areas; to the degree that residential differentiation does exist, Swedish cities tend to follow the preindustrial
residential pattern, with the higher classes living close to the city center and
the poorer classes inhabiting the suburbs. Cities in the United States, on
the other hand, are noted for their great residential segregation, with the
poor in the central city and the wealthy in the suburbs.

Metropolitan form in Britain falls between the forms of the United
States and Sweden in virtually every important dimension, with, if anything, a slight leaning in the Swedish direction. The typical dwelling units
in British urban places are terraced and semidetached single-family houses,
which generates urban densities between those of the other two nations.
Also, Britain is midway between Sweden and the United States in degree of
urban containment, use of public transportation, preservation of downtown areas, and residential differentiation of social classes.

How is one to account for these rather surprising differences in urban
form among societies that are alike in so many other important respects?
What specific historical and contemporary structural factors combine to
determine the metropolitan form characteristic of each society? The dissimilarities will be discussed under five headings: housing density and
dwelling type; means of transportation; urban containment and urban
sprawl; the function of city centers; and residential differentiation.

### Housing Density and Dwelling Type

From an American perspective, high-density apartment living is associated with poverty, a scarcity of land, and the era of urban development
before the automobile. Such conditions are found mainly in the older cities
of the eastern United States. By the same token, the single-family house is
associated with wealth, abundant land, and twentieth-century development around the automobile, features especially of the West and new
South in the United States. While these factors certainly play a role in
generating housing densities, the cross-national comparison demonstrates
that their role is not a fully determinant one. Sweden has far more available
land for urban development than Britain, is much wealthier than Britain,
has had about twice that nation's per capita ownership of private cars, and
underwent the process of urban development at a later stage of history.
These factors suggest that, compared to Britain, Sweden should have much
lower housing densities, yet the opposite is the case.

Indeed, with the lowest national population density and the highest per capita wealth and automobile ownership in Western Europe, Sweden has nearly the highest density of housing development within urban areas. Britain, the first nation to become urbanized with a very high national population density and now one of the lowest levels of per capita income, has Western Europe's lowest urban-housing densities. What the comparison of Britain and Sweden points up are the additional important factors of history and geography (what might loosely be called tradition) and the role of governments in directing the process of urbanization, sometimes in directions opposed to those preferred by most individuals.

That Great Britain has the lowest urban-housing densities in Europe is in large part the result of its history and geography. Unlike most continental countries, Britain has not been invaded by a foreign power since the Norman invasion of 1066; it is insulated and protected by its island position, separated from the Continent by a body of water. Many aspects of British society and culture, relative to its European counterparts, can be attributed to the long years of independence and autonomous self-development. Britain's early movement away from serfdom and its early development of parliamentary democracy without the violent revolutions of the Continent have no doubt played an important part in developing distinct cultural traits.

Rural dwellers the world over, with very few exceptions, live in detached houses. The multifamily building comes into being with the development of towns and cities. In the revival of European town life in the Middle Ages the new urban places tended to be, as much as anything, places of defense; in form they were a greatly expanded version of the medieval castle. Almost a defining characteristic of the early towns, distinguishing them from agricultural villages, was the presence of a defensive wall with military fortification. Because space within the wall was very limited, housing was forced up in density as the towns grew (although urban growth also occurred through successive expansions of the town wall). Thus the citizens of continental European towns became apartment dwellers, a tradition that has continued long after the original defensive needs ended. Indeed, dense cities today are more vulnerable in contemporary warfare.

Although Britain had its complement of walled towns in the Middle Ages, security was not such a major consideration in urban development, and cities like London soon spread out at densities lower than anything found on the Continent in urban places of equivalent population.[3] This is a major respect in which London has been called, from a continental perspective, a "unique city."[4] Other British cities (Scottish cities are an exception) show the same preference for ground-level over high- and medium-rise accommodation.

Today the association of Britain with ground-level housing is a close one in the European mind. The association is surely enhanced by the British proclivity for gardening, and love, in general, for country life. The British climate and geography are well suited both to lush gardens and to the pursuit of country living at its richest. With a mild climate, neither too hot in summer nor in winter too cold, a long growing season, and a felicitous mixture of sunshine and rain, gardens thrive. So too does country living in a benign environment, with a landscape of great natural grace and beauty, accessibility, and malleability.

While the continental aristocracy was attracted to the urban drawing room, where it generated a culture rich in those qualities stemming from the free interplay of minds found only in cities, the English aristocracy was in farm and field, often attending to the serious business of agriculture. English culture came to be oriented to themes more associated with rural than with urban living: individualism, practicality and efficiency; the self-help and independence of the rural yeomanry; love of the land. English artistocracy is still today based heavily on land ownership, and even more, on the life-style of the country gentleman. The aristocrat's London town house is typically not the main but an auxiliary place of residence, merely a dwelling for use during the work week.

Owing to the principle of upper-class cultural emulation (or, if it is preferred, downward cultural diffusion), the practices and cultural style of a society's upper class have widespread ramifications for lower social classes. The individualism and desire for privacy, the love of gardening and of the land, and the lure of country life are strong in the minds of the British people as a whole. These themes make up an ongoing cultural pressure for low-density community forms, forms that promote a realization of the British adage "A man's house is his castle."

This cultural explanation takes one a long way in accounting for the reasons that British cities so significantly differ in density and dwelling type from their continental counterparts. But such an explanation is not as convincing in the analysis of Britain's differences from the United States, the latter having many of the cultural traits of its former colonial ruler. New York is much more densely settled than London, yet it is an exception. The other major eastern cities are comparable in density to London, despite having less public open space. But most other cities of the United States are places of single-family homes, many of which are detached. One can argue that the cultural themes of individualism, independence, and landedness are even stronger in American than in British culture. This argument gains cogency from the vastly different histories of the two nations. The United States had no medieval walled towns. It even had relatively few agricultural villages, urban development having sprung from a society made up of independent farmsteads, people living physically apart from one another in semiwilderness conditions. Would such people, when brought to the city, choose to live in anything but a detached house? It is also true that the availability of land, wealth, and the automobile must all be brought into a full accounting of U.S. and British differences. Yet there is one other factor that is equally significant, if not more so, in accounting for British-American dissimilarities: the role of government in urban development.

In the United States, government has taken a relatively limited role in the process of urban development,[5] as in almost every other sphere of American life. The rights of private landowners to use their land as they see fit, for example, are much more extensive than in Europe. And the government has not intervened as actively in the housing market. Urban housing has been supplied mainly by profit-making entrepreneurs, and the housing has been of the type preferred by the buyers—single-family housing on large lots. The poor have not been well served by this process and the resulting cities and metropolitan areas have not been, as a whole, environments that people particularly want or like. In Britain, on the other hand, government intervention has generated more low-cost housing of higher quality (much of which is at relatively high density), and the intervention has created metropolitan environments that on the whole must be rated higher in public amenity than those of the United States.

The role of government action can be seen even more clearly in the analysis of housing density differences between Britain and Sweden. The Swedish government has seemingly pushed the nation toward a style of housing that would not otherwise have become dominant.

Sweden may be classified as a continental European nation, in which the most dominant foreign cultural influences have been France and Germany. Yet in many respects Sweden has been in the same position with reference to the continent as Britain. Like Britain, Sweden is geographically isolated from continental Europe by a body of water. This has prevented foreign political dominance for centuries. It was only Denmark that ever gained hegemony over Sweden, and that early in its history. Unlike Britain, Sweden has not even been engaged in a foreign war since the early nineteenth century. Sweden stayed on the sidelines during the great continental upheavals of the eighteenth and nineteenth centuries and the great struggles of the twentieth century. Thus conditions of peace and security are even more characteristic of Sweden than of Britain.

Sweden's history of settlement is more similar to that of the United States and to a lesser extent Britain's than it is to the rest of Europe. Sweden was a rural nation until the end of the nineteenth century, and, after the breakup of villages and the farm enclosures of the eighteenth century, the peasants lived mostly on separate farmsteads. Rural villages were much less common than in England, as were walled towns and cities. When urbanization came, people moved from independent farmsteads to towns in a way similar to the American pattern. The love of the land, and for the rural countryside, remains every bit as strong in Sweden as in Britain. Indeed, the Swedish male aristocrat has long had a strong admiration for the English country gentleman, and has tended despite a much less privileged position to emulate many aspects of his life-style.

When these same cultural factors, which were used to account for Britain's low urban density, are added to the factors of Sweden's much greater availability of land, wealth, and automobile ownership and its more recent urbanization, how is one to explain Sweden's urban densities, among the highest in Western Europe? The answer lies in Sweden's greater (and earlier) use of government controls over the urbanization process.

The Stockholm city planning office dates back to 1637, and has functioned more or less continuously since that time.[6] As in Britain, the government took on the role of housing provision early in the twentieth century. But Swedish local authorities took an even more significant step at the same time by buying up a great deal of the open land surrounding their muncipalitites, land that later would be used for urban growth. Thus the stage was set for the highly planned development of the cities and towns that followed World War II.

Before the war, Sweden's urban housing densities were quite similar to Britain's. From the last part of the nineteenth century Sweden's cities showed ample evidence of the suburbanization process common to capitalist societies: the wealthy moving to large suburban houses, often ranged along suburban railway lines. And, as early as 1905, government-sponsored schemes were enacted to provide single-family suburban housing for lower-middle- and even working-class families. These schemes were strongly influenced by the "garden cities" movement in England at the time. But as the Swedish government became more active in the housing market, spurred on by very serious urban housing shortages, the construction of multi-family structures predominated, especially during the 1930s after the Social Democratic party came to power.

During World War II, Sweden's government planners had both the time and the stimulus, due to a continuing housing shortage and the prospects of massive postwar urbanization, to consider carefully the kind of urban housing that would be best. (The Ministry of Reconstruction in Britain performed the same role.) Taking many aspects of city life and form into consideration—the problems of the inner city, problems of efficiency in transportation, and problems of housing segregation—and realizing the paramount need to build as many dwelling units as fast and as economically as possible, they decided to continue Sweden's prewar urban tradition of apartment living.

Some opinion was ranged against apartment housing in favor of the British and American alternatives, but the debate was mainly among planners and the powerful groups with whom they most came into contact: business and industry, and in this case the public transportation bodies. Because it was a debate among the elite and the powerful, the housing desires of individual residents were not a serious input.[7] Indeed, a public opinion poll at the time in Stockholm showed that a majority of people wanted single-family houses.[8] Needless to say, the people did not get them.

So Swedish housing densities are a planners' alternative, and for better or worse, Swedish cities are planners' cities. In this sense Swedish urban development is much more akin to that of the Eastern European socialist countries than it is to the United States. There are, however, factors that generate high urban densities in Sweden apart from the wishes of government officials and planners. Because housing must be heavily insulated against the cold and harsh climate, the construction cost of a single-family house is higher than elsewhere, certainly than in Britain, where home insulation is minimal. And the long winter and short growing season considerably reduce the utility of one of the real advantages of ground-level housing, namely, the private garden. Instead of having one spacious house and garden, Swedes have developed a tradition of two-dwelling living: an urban apartment for the winter months, and a vacation and weekend cottage to enjoy during the long days of summer. (Twenty percent of Swedish households own second homes, the highest rate in the world, and many more have access to such homes.) Finally, Sweden has the world's smallest household size.[9] For one- and two-person households, which make up more than 50 percent of all households, apartment living is often to be preferred.

## Means of Transport

High-density cities rely more heavily on public, mass transportation than less densely populated ones. In the United States, public transportation is more important in San Francisco than it is in Los Angeles, and more important in New York than it is in San Francisco. There are two underlying reasons for the relationship. First, enough private cars to supply transportation needs simply do not "fit" in dense cities. Second, at very low densities, public transportation becomes very inefficient; the private car must be relied on. If the citizens of Stockholm owned and operated as many private vehicles as the citizens of Los Angeles, Stockholm would become unmanageable chaos. The form of the city of Los Angeles is made possible by the private car; it would not be possible without it. High housing densities therefore make the use of private cars problematical; low densities demand such use.

This relationship accounts for many of the differences between urban transport systems in Britain and the United States. The higher densities in British cities make mass transportation more efficient; the lower densities of American cities make it less efficient and the automobile more necessary. Thus there are 3.8 persons per vehicle in Britain compared with only 2.0 in the United States. But the British own fewer cars partly because they cannot afford to buy more; it is not that they do not want more. And British densities certainly make the car a distinct convenience, if not always an absolute necessity. One could add that, in view of the densities of English cities, and the prevalence of nineteenth-century street widths and patterns, it is a good thing that the British people are not able to afford more private vehicles. Even with Britain's present levels of car ownership, the traffic congestion in sections of the larger British cities often rivals that found in the United States, if indeed it does not surpass it. Moreover many historic townscapes have been irrecoverably damaged by adaptation to heavy traffic and car parking.

In certain respects Sweden does not follow the density-transportation relationship we have been describing. With very high densities, it also has Europe's highest rate of automobile ownership (2.8 persons per vehicle). This requires explanation. Despite high automobile purchase taxes, high gasoline prices and high parking fees, it seems clear that Sweden has a high per capita rate of automobile ownership because its citizens can afford it; Sweden is a wealthy nation. That Swedes own fewer cars than Americans, who have a lower per capita income, is a testament, however, to the high costs of car ownership in Sweden (deliberately set high by the government), to higher densities and hence shorter travel distances and greater parking problems, and to the availability of public transport. In areas of excellent public transportation, such as Stockholm, automobile ownership is well below the national average. And it is probable, although precise data are not available, that automobile use, apart from ownership, is low in Sweden's cities, compared to the cities where public transport is less adequate. Swedes tend to use the automobile less during weekdays for work and shopping, reserving its use for longer trips on the weekend. Thus the high densities of Swedish cities make the automobile less a necessity than a luxury; but it is a luxury that the Swedes can afford while at the same time limiting its use.

Sweden points up another important aspect of the relationship between housing density and transportation: transportation can generate housing density as well as vice versa. Of all the factors involved in the decision of Stockholm to build high-density suburbs following World War II, public transport networks appear to have been the most significant.[10] Stockholm's planners knew that postwar Stockholm would function much better with an extensive subway system. They also reckoned that the subway would be most used and hence most efficient and economic if homes were concentrated around the subway stations, so people would be able to get to the trains on foot or by public transport. As a consequence, it is reasonable to say that Stockholm's high residential densities stem in large part from the desire to make mass transportation efficient. Without mass transportation, the pressures for high-density living are considerably less compelling.

## Urban Containment and Urban Sprawl

To the eyes of an American visitor, one of the most unusual things about many European cities is that they have a distinct boundary. Despite their density and size, whether high or low, large or small, they come to a sudden end (or have an abrupt beginning); city and noncity are two quite separate landscapes. In contrast, American cities and towns gradually dissolve into the countryside. Houses appear at ever lower densities, finally ending with the last isolated roadside house (although perhaps nearby is a house marking the beginning of the next town, as is the case with those multi-metropolitan regions sometimes referred to as megalopolises).

The American urban development pattern may be called "natural" in that it just happens through the normal course of the buying and selling of real estate and the construction of houses, shops, and workplaces. No one plans it that way, and no one tries to stop it. In American cities there are some controls over peripheral development, zoning controls over the use of land, and subdivision controls over the placement and character of new housing, for example, but such controls are relatively weak, not difficult to circumvent, and because the peripheral areas are typically under the jurisdiction of a variety of local governments, which administer the controls, the pattern of the controls is not organized and the effect is not consistent.

The weakness of the controls can be seen by comparing the form of cities that have public controls, such as Los Angeles, with the form of a city such as Houston, which has no zoning regulations and few public controls over land use of any other kind.[11] To the average onlooker, the cities appear virtually identical in form; it is a form dictated by private developers making decisions about how best to use land they own, *best* meaning the maximization of their own profits. Land close to cities is more in demand, therefore more costly to buy and own. The developer must build at high densities, thus gaining a better return. Land at a greater remove is less expensive and may be built on at lower densities. Thus densities decline by distance from the center of a city, with of course the distortions of subcities, topography, and transport routes. As more people want to or must live in the vicinity of cities, the cities accommodate them by growing outward, taking over land previously used for agriculture.

The cities and towns of Britain were built much the same way until the early part of this century, when town planning legislation began to appear. Especially important was the national Town and Country Planning Act of 1932, which gave local government many new powers to control land development. Under the act, cities and towns across Britain began to control such urban forms as ribbon (or strip) development, the urban development that grows up along both sides of transport arteries that interconnect urban places. Most of the ribbon development in Britain today dates from before 1932.

During World War II even more stringent national legislation was devised and later enacted in the early postwar years. It was decided to control further growth of large cities by zoning a permanent "green belt" around them, within which the land would be maintained in a rural state. All new development within the green belt was to be forbidden, and changes of existing uses within the green belt were to be strictly limited. Part of the new housing and other facilities for a growing urban population were to be diverted beyond the green belts into new towns and the carefully planned expansion of old towns.

Some of the green belt legislation was not fully enacted until as late as 1955. Even after that, strong economic and population pressures (the planners seriously underestimated Britain's postwar population growth) caused green belts to be violated in some instances. Yet it cannot be denied that the legislation has had a most significant effect on the containment of British cities; the effect is clearly visible all across Britain.[12]

What has Britain really accomplished by this planning feat? Clearly the appearance, if not the way of life, of the rural countryside has been kept remarkably intact. And many Britons have found themselves comfortably living in new and expanded towns rather than large cities, a situation that for most seems to be desired. But there are also drawbacks, the nature and extent of which were carefully analyzed by Marion Clawson and Peter Hall in a book comparing the U.S. and British postwar urbanization experience.[13] Chief among the drawbacks is congestion of the contained cities. Because outward growth was limited, land and house prices have risen and densities have tended to rise. Many suburbanites must live in high-rise housing on the edge of the green belt, and shop in older urban centers that have become congested by the automobile. In addition, employment has not decentralized as rapidly as housing; urban dwellers make a longer journey to work that sometimes requires crossing the green belt back into the city. Moreover, in the stagnant economy there is now competition from the cities to keep industry rather than cause increased unemployment through further loss of jobs to the suburbs.

Although it is not an unmixed blessing, and it has been subjected to severe criticism, British green belt policy is unlikely to be abandoned. In many ways it has merely molded British cities and towns more into the shape of those in Sweden and other European countries. Swedish towns are also sharply contained at their edges, but this is less the result of a major instrument of national legislation than of the day-to-day local planning practices of Swedish municipalities. Due to a longer and stronger tradition of public planning and control over the use of land, Swedish urbanization is even more orderly and efficient than is Britain's. But Swedish planning has been aided by a slower population growth and a larger supply of land.

The ascription of stronger control over land in Europe and the greater capacity of European governments to plan begs the question of why the two governments are so much more powerful than the U.S. government. Why is land treated as a private possession in the United States, the use and disposition of which rest largely with the owner, while in Europe it is a public resource, whose use and disposition are heavily determined by government? It is the United States that is out of line with the rest of the advanced world in this respect, not vice versa, and thus it is the United States that must be explained. It would be both facile and obvious to say that the main reason is the frontier past, when land was plentiful and free for the taking, and once taken, stoutly defended as an extension of a person's worth and the product of a person's toil. This is clearly partly the case, but individual rights in land in the United States are much more extensive than in countries such as Canada, which had a similar frontier past and where land is just as plentiful.

The lack of public planning and control of land in the United States is just one part of a general pattern of weak government activity in almost every of area life, from welfare and health through national economic planning. In political values Americans believe more in limited government, local autonomy, self-help, and the protection of individual rights. At the same time, the nation's great diversity of population, in relation to regional, racial, and national origins, renders collective decision making more difficult. Underlying solidarity and cohesion are limited, making agreement on common policies a more problematic task.

At the other extreme, Sweden's homogeneity, geographic isolation, and peace have fostered strong government that is widely accepted by the people, even people of a conservative persuasion.[14] Not only is agreement on public action easier to achieve in Sweden but trust in government and in government officials is higher than in the United States. This means that Swedish citizens are less involved in controversial decisions than Americans are. They are less politicized, less willing, as ordinary citizens, to "interfere" in the political process, and much more willing to leave political decisions to elected representatives. The result is public policies that are more in the public interest, or at least in the interest of the politicians, civil servants, and experts who make up the governments, than in the immediate and short-run interest of the electorate.

In few areas do the conflicts between the rights of private individuals and the needs of the community show up more clearly than in land use and planning, for a person's private use of property may be little related to public need, and public use of that property all too often is decidely at odds with the wishes of the owner. Which is the higher value, individual right or community need? The Swedish and American sociopolitical systems have come out with different answers to this question.[15]

With individualism a more strongly imbedded cultural value, the British political system lies slightly to the right of the Swedish, that is, in the direction of the United States system. Public planning did not develop as early as it did in Sweden, and it did not develop with quite the same rigor and extensiveness. Britain's more limited planning powers, however, were partially offset by the evolution in that nation of a relatively unified philosophy of planning.

Although the agreement on planning goals is considerably less today than it once was, Britain's planners throughout most of this century have been in surprising unanimity in their views of the desirable urban structure. The philosophy was set forth in its clearest and most influential form by Ebenezer Howard, a lay planner whose book *Garden Cities of Tomorrow*[16] launched the British New Towns movement and molded planning thought for decades to come. In reaction to the excesses and squalor of Victorian cities, Howard argued for severe limitations on the further growth and spread of large cities, and the channeling of people into modestly sized, relatively self-contained New Towns, with the preservation of permanent agricultural land between the New Towns and the parent city. This is precisely the policy the British government adopted in 1946, many years after Howard's death, although in practice in did not achieve all that Howard had wished for. In particular only a limited number of people were actually housed in New Towns; about 3 percent of postwar housing units were built in them.[17]

## Function of City Centers

How can European city centers be so vital, thriving, and well preserved, when those in the United States are, with a few exceptions, a national disgrace? Even those few exceptions—New York and San Francisco leap quickly to mind—are ridden with slums and crime, and beset by financial crises.

The fate of U.S. city centers relies heavily upon the dictates of the real estate market, which in turn reflects changes in the economic and social structure. First, with rising incomes, private cars, and a relatively uncontrolled market in land, wealthier people were prompted to follow their desires and move to the suburbs. To live in a semirural environment of safety and privacy, away from the much less salubrious environment of the industrial city, they were willing to pay the costs of a single-family house, plus one or more private automobiles, and then commute back to the city. Next industry and commerce moved out; industry to achieve space to expand, and commerce to be near the customers. The movement of industry and shops made the suburbs all the more desirable, and the suburbanite had no further need to go to the city. A familiar cycle set in: the more the wealthier classes, the jobs, and the shops left the central city, the less desirable it became, causing still more people and facilities to leave. The city-center vacuum was gradually filled by racial and other minority groups, members of the large underclass, people with poor education, very low incomes, and few job prospects. In some American cities today welfare payments support nearly half of all residents, in large part children, women, and the elderly. The market had dictated a declining function for dense city areas, built up originally in an age without the automobile and without widely distributed personal wealth. Only the underclass who cannot leave stay.

How is it that Swedish cities in particular, and European cities in general, have so far escaped the destructive impact of these social and economic trends? The answer seems to be largely because their governments have acted to counter those trends that detract from the city, and at the same time to stimulate the maintenance of city centers as desirable places to live. The policies outlined in the discussions of housing density, transportation, and urban containment have been particularly crucial. By minimizing the development of single-family houses around Stockholm, for example, and partially suppressing the use of the automobile, Swedish government efforts have severely short-circuited the suburbanization trend so common in the United States. At the same time, measures have been taken to make Stockholm more attractive, for example reducing densities, improving retail services, and providing such public facilities as parks and recreation areas and efficient transportation. Thus the wealthy choose to stay in town; for many it is the most desirable place to live.

The suburban areas that were built near Stockholm, and there are just as many as in comparable cities elsewhere, were designed in such a way as to enhance the center rather than to detract from it. Indeed, there are those who say the postwar planners had in mind the future of central Stockholm more than a desirable suburban environment when they planned the suburbs. Good commuter transportation, made more efficient by the density and layout of suburban housing, promoted within the city the continuing provision of both jobs and shopping while simultaneously minimizing the automobile's inner-city use. Compared to other European cities, downtown Stockholm is much less dominated by the private car, despite Sweden's higher rate of car ownership.

Sweden's urban centers today are probably the most suited to residential use of any such centers in the world. Because they lack variety, a rich street life, bars and bistros, and late-evening entertainment—features that cause young people from all over the world to flock to European cities—they are not necessarily the most exciting places to visit. But in meeting the needs and desires of permanent residents of many different age groups, they come close to providing an optimum balance between the costs and benefits of urban environments. They provide in good measure the proximity to cultural activities, specialty shopping, and jobs that the city dweller desires while at the same time maintaining a high standard of safety, cleanliness, transport efficiency, educational facilities and quiet—features sorely lacking in many cities. Indeed, such an urban environment, suitable for old as well as young, families as well as single people, poor as well as rich, has all but disappeared from the American scene.

In Britain, with the great exception of London, city centers are less vital, dominant, and habitable than they are in Sweden (yet they are more like city centers in Sweden than the United States). There are several reasons for this. Britain has had to pay a price for being the first urban nation. The legacy of Victorian cities still remains and the task of making such places habitable by modern standards far surpasses the problem of urban renewal in Sweden. Long ago the well-to-do left the centers of such cities as Leeds, Sheffield, and Liverpool; it is difficult and impractical to bring them back. In addition, Britain has encouraged a lower density form of suburbanization than has Sweden. This has tended to undermine public transportation, foster the use of automobiles in downtown areas, and spread people out at such a distance that the center loses its hold. Finally, Britain's depressed economic state has not permitted as much downtown renewal as the nation would like. Public services tend to be undermaintained, and in the most deteriorated areas, such as Liverpool, whole neighborhoods lie vacant, cleared of slums but without new uses. On the other hand, there is a sense in which greater prosperity in Britain could create more problems for that nation's downtown areas, because more money leads to more automobile ownership and use, increased pressure for low-density suburbanization, and a drop-off in demand for older inner-city housing, whose chief merit is that it is cheap.

## Residential Differentiation

Although few foreign visitors may realize it, one of the most notable features of Swedish cities is the spatial distribution of their population. It is taken for granted in the United States that the poor live in the city and the wealthy in the suburbs. Yet in Sweden the reverse is largely the case: the pattern of preindustrial cities is continued in an advanced industrial society. How has this pattern persisted and why is it so different from that in the United States?

The reasons have been included in the discussions above. Through government action, city centers have been so well maintained that they have very high land values; an in-town environment both has a continuing attraction for, and can mainly be afforded by, the better off. (In the United States this situation can still be found in limited areas, such as the East Side of Manhattan, and parts of Boston and San Francisco.) Because the higher classes dominate the inner city, Sweden's poor are forced to the suburbs, where, with the help of government subsidies, they can afford the recently built housing. It is a feature of Swedish life that the poor live in newer housing than the rich. In view of this pattern, it is apparent why Sweden has so few areas that could be called slums. Indeed, if Sweden could be said to have slums, they are to be found in the suburbs—in some of the new housing estates to which the poor have been directed in relatively large numbers.

Thus many of the same conditions that led to the spatial distribution of the population in preindustrial cities still prevail in Sweden's advanced-industrial urban places. The wealthy still command the city centers, which are close to jobs and shopping and are well supplied with facilities and services. The poor are forced to the less desirable (though modern) city outskirts.

Swedish urban communities also differ substantially from those in the United States in the degree to which the population groupings are inter-mixed within a single neighborhood, modifying to some extent the residential pattern described above. Many poor continue to live in the city and many wealthy live in suburbs. Also relatively intermixed are age groups, families with nonfamilies, and racial and other minority groups.

The pronounced residential segregation of these social groupings in the United States stems initially from the great diversity of the population, and the looseness of nationwide social and cultural ties. The United States is preeminently a nation of subcultures, and this is reflected in its residential patterns. People seek (and in some cases are forced) to live with their own kind, those who share their subculture, whether that subculture is based on race, class, nationality, or stage of the life cycle. In the presence of a weak societal culture the subcultures are a major source of meaning and identity.

Subcultural residential segregation is made possible by the great amount of available space, and by the way in which a private real estate market is able to serve this goal.

Sweden, by contrast, is a very homogeneous society; until recently even its foreign immigrants have been mostly from neighboring countries and thus relatively easily assimilated. And due to greater equality in the distribution of income, subcultural differences based on social class are less than in the United States. Moreover, Swedish culture is still highly integrated and intact, reducing the need for subcultures as a source of meaning and identity.

Not only is the cultural pressure for subcultural segregation less in Sweden than the United States but much more active public measures are taken to prevent social segregation in residential areas. Persons in financial need are given housing subsidies, which expand the range of neighborhoods in which such persons may live. Public housing and privately constructed housing are often placed side by side, leading to still further intermixing of income groups. New residential areas are built with a wide range of housing types and sizes, so that young and old who typically desire small units are intermixed with households, such as families with children, requiring more space. Immigrants are as an act of policy dispersed to available housing as they arrive, so dispersed in fact that immigrant groups sometimes express the desire for more segregation, in the search for a greater feeling of security in an alien culture. In all of these ways the Swedish government has attempted to foster, of course without complete success, the integration of many different peoples in local neighborhoods.

Britain again falls between the two nations in its degree of residential segregation, and also in its metropolitan distribution of class groupings. Its city centers have not been entirely given over to the poor, as is the case in so many American cities. In fact, central London is heavily occupied by the wealthy, and cities like Birmingham have areas of the wealthy located near the center. Inner-city land values remain very high, but a backlog of deteriorated, old housing and a delayed rehabilitation program have left large pockets of slums in many cities, slums that are partially counterbalanced by the creation of many working-class housing estates in the newer suburban districts. Britain does not have the great number of immigrants and minority groups that the United States has, but it has more than Sweden, and these groups typically find themselves heavily concentrated in inner-city areas, in line with the American pattern. A policy of deliberate dispersal of immigrant groups like that used in Sweden has been ruled illegal discrimination under the Race Relations Acts in Britain.

The existence of a strong working-class subculture in inner cities in Britain has been well documented. This class is still quite prominent in many British inner cities, as it is in some eastern cities in the United States, but it is gradually being eroded through the arrival in the old working-class neighborhoods of new immigrant groups, and through the movement of workers to suburban public housing estates, even to New Towns and expanded smaller towns.[18] The outward movement of workers has led to considerable class mixing in the suburban areas, far more than is found in the United States. However, class mixing in Britain is more limited than in Sweden at the neighborhood and the block levels. Though nearly a third of British housing is publicly rented, it is not usually intermixed with private housing. Some attempts are being made to reverse this in new buildings, but the basic pattern of class segregation is already set.

## Conclusion

These, then, are brief explanations for the outstanding dissimilarities of metropolitan form found among the three advanced industrial societies. In addition to the variations in history, geography, and culture, which shape urban form in ways not always realized, the use of governmental power in planning and in land use control is a most important factor. Government action appears truly to be a potent force in determining the shape of cities. Although not at all surprising to Europeans, this conclusion needs to be reemphasized in the United States, where there is a tendency to forget or ignore the fact that advanced industrial societies do have some capacity to shape urbanization into collectively desired forms. These societies are not inherently held captive by impersonal forces associated with economic growth and residential mobility.

## Notes

1. For example, D.I. Scargill, *The Form of Cities* (London: Bell & Hyman, 1979); R.L. Johnston, *Urban Residential Patterns* (London: G. Bell & Sons, 1971); D.W.G. Timms, *The Urban Mosaic* (Cambridge: Cambridge University Press, 1971); B.T. Robson, *Urban Analysis* (Cambridge: Cambridge University Press, 1969); Kent P. Schwirian, *Comparative Urban Structure* (Lexington, Mass.: Heath, 1974); and Brian J.L. Berry and J.D. Kasarda, *Contemporary Urban Ecology* (New York: Macmillan, 1977).
2. See, for example, David M. Gordon, "Capitalist Development and the History of American Cities," in *Marxism and the Metropolis*, ed. W.K. Tabb and L. Sawers (New York: Oxford University Press, 1978); Manuel Castells, *The Urban Question* (Cambridge: MIT Press, 1977); David Harvey, *Social Justice and the City* (Baltimore: John Hopkins University Press, 1973); and M. Dear and A.J. Scott, eds., *Urbanization and Urban Planning in Capitalist Society* (London: Methuen, 1981).
3. See J.R. Mellor, *Urban Sociology in an Urbanized Society* (London: Routledge & Kegan Paul, 1977); and E. Cherry, *Urban Change and Planning* (Henley-on-Thames: G.T. Foulis, 1972).

72    **Private Pleasure, Public Plight**

4. Stein Eiler Rasmussen, *London: The Unique City* (London: Jonathan Cape, 1948).
5. A.J. Heidenheimer et al., *Comparative Public Policy* (London: St. Martin's, 1975); and Marion Clawson and P. Hall, *Planning and Urban Growth* (Baltimore: Johns Hopkins University Press, 1973).
6. E. Ödmann and G. Dahlberg, *Urbanization in Sweden* (Stockholm: Allmänna Förlaget, 1970).
7. David Popenoe, *The Suburban Environment: Sweden and the U.S.* (Chicago: University of Chicago Press, 1977), pp. 40-51.
8. City of Stockholm, *City Plan* (Stockholm, 1952), p. 167.
9. J.T. Coppock, ed., *Second Homes: Curse or Blessing?* (Oxford: Pergamon Press, 1977), p. 155. Average household size in Sweden is currently estimated to be about 2.3.
10. G.Sidenbladh, "Stockholm: A Planned City," in *Cities: Their Origin, Growth and Human Impact* (San Francisco: W.H. Freeman, 1973).
11. J. Delafons, *Land Use Controls in the U.S.* (Cambridge, Mass: Joint Center for Urban Studies, 1969); Bernard H. Siegan, *Land Use without Zoning* (Lexington, Mass: Lexington Books, 1972); and Joe R. Feagin, "Metropolis and Mega-structures: Houston in the Era of Late Capitalism," paper presented at 77th meeting of the American Sociological Association, 1982.
12. Peter Hall, *Urban and Regional Planning* (New York: Penguin, 1975), ch.7.
13. Clawson and Hall, *Planning and Urban Growth*.
14. R.F. Tomasson, *Sweden: Prototype of Modern Society* (New York: Random House, 1970), ch. 2; and Thomas J. Anton, *Administered Politics* (Boston: Martinus Nijhoff, 1980).
15. Popenoe, *Suburban Environment*.
16. Ebenezer Howard, *Garden Cities of Tomorrow* (Cambridge: MIT Press, 1965 [1902]).
17. Clawson and Hall, *Planning and Urban Growth*, p. 215.
18. N. Deakin and C. Ungerson, *Leaving London: Planned Mobility and the Inner City* (London: Heinemann, 1977).

# PART III
# LIFE

# 5

# Everyday Life in the Metropolitan Area

In view of the striking environmental differences discussed in the previous chapter, it would be surprising indeed if the everyday lives of metropolitan dwellers were not shaped accordingly, if we were not to find substantial dissimilarities among the three nations in the life-styles of metropolitan residents. There are some notable dissimilarities, as this chapter will make clear, but many similarities also exist that attest the common economic and cultural conditions in which the citizens of these nations find themselves.

A discussion of life-styles easily can lend itself to caricature and stereotype. There are no two people, however similar in sociocultural characteristics, who have life-styles identical in every respect. But that there are substantial life-style differences among cultures cannot be denied, and that one can identify typical life-styles associated with different cultural settings is more than just the assertion of the observant tourist. Indeed, the concept of life-style has gained great currency within sociology over the past decade because it represents a kind of summary product of social and cultural forces in a society as those forces affect individual behavior.[1]

Definitionally, *style* refers to "the meaningful and distinctive manner of expression characteristic of an object or person." When applied to a human life, the concept of style has been operationalized by sociologists to refer to the allocation of time, money, and energy that an individual makes to social roles, activities, and patterns of living.[2] Our interest here is in the typical ways that metropolitan adults allocate these scarce resources in their everyday pursuit of the major life activities: home care, working, socializing, social participation, shopping, and leisure. In matters of interpretation, I have tried to portray the life-styles of each country as they generally appear from the perspective of foreign observers rather than in terms of any absolute or universal standard. Despite all my efforts to set aside my own value judgments, they have not been removed fully from the discussion that follows.

Within metropolitan areas, life-styles differ in terms of three main sociological variables: social class, ethnicity, and stage of the life cycle. Because the concern of this book is with central tendencies and typicality, the focus of discussion will be on the life-style of the metropolitan "middle mass" in each nation: middle-, lower-middle-, and upper-working-class people who inhabit, in American terms, neither the metropolitan center nor its far periphery but rather live in the "outer city" and "inner suburbs," the vast expanses of residential neighborhoods that geographically dominate the metropolitan scene. Where appropriate, however, the main ways in which characteristic life-styles of the lower and upper classes differ from that of the middle mass will also be suggested.

Ethnicity is an especially potent variable in accounting for life-style differences. The variations in normative content associated with religion, race, and national origin can overwhelm the variations connected with social-class level, and seem especially prominent in an ethnically heterogeneous society like the United States. But ethnicity poses a special problem in international comparisons. There is no group comparable in Sweden to the American blacks, nothing quite comparable in the other countries to the Finnish minority in Sweden, and so on. The ethnic heterogeneity of each society indeed plays a fundamental role in the character of that society's metropolitan life, but for a comparison of typical life-styles it is best to overlook the ethnic variations within a single society and to strive for common denominators.

Stage of the life cycle also seriously complicates the picture. Possibly no other variable is as strong in affecting the way in which everyday lives are structured than the stage of life, a combination of age and family situation. It is obvious that the life of a teenager is very different from that of a retired person; that the life of an unmarried career woman is not the same as that of the mother of six children.

At one time in history, virtually every person lived within the confines of a nuclear or extended family. In advanced societies we are approaching the time when fewer than half of all households consist of families, the remainder being made up of a single individual or several unrelated individuals. And although most persons in a society once may have proceeded through the "normal" stages of childhood, marriage, parenthood, and old age, a growing number are now skipping the intermediate stages, particularly insofar as children of one's own are concerned. How should this great diversity be handled? For each society we shall begin by sketching the life-style of what remains the ideal if not the most common household— that consisting of husband, wife, and children. Within that type, a most important differentiating factor is whether or not the wife works. After sketching that type, we shall do what was done for social class—show the way that other life stages and household types vary from the norm, especially households with no children and persons living alone. These kinds of households are to be an important dimension of the analysis to follow in Part IV.

Everyday life takes place in a residential environment. Providing both opportunities and constraints, the environment plays no small role in shaping the lives contained within it. Drawing on the analysis in Part II, the characteristic residential environments in each nation will be summarized below, together with some of the principal life-environment interrelationships.

As in the case of the discussion of metropolitan form, there is a logic that dictates first a presentation of the Swedish life-style, then the American, both of these representing poles of a continuum, and finally the English as a point somewhere midway between the two. Thus we turn first to the Swedish case.

### Sweden: Private Lives in an Orderly Environment

The characteristic metropolitan Swedish adult lives in a three- or four-room apartment in a low-rise walk-up apartment building (what Americans refer to as a garden apartment building) set in an urbanized area of relatively abundant public and private facilities, including parks and playgrounds, small shops, and day care centers. The buildings are spaciously arranged so that densities are relatively low, yet the floor space of the dwelling unit itself is also quite low by American standards, having perhaps only half the square footage of the U.S. single-family house. Moreover, the Swedes have no private garage or private yard.

The standard of amenities within the apartment is quite high, however, with most of the labor-saving devices found in the American home except perhaps for a washer-dryer and a dishwasher. Swedes own one television set but seldom two (there are 348 sets per thousand persons in Sweden compared to 571/1000 in the United States).[3] Aside from some of the big appliances, the Swedish apartments are as well equipped as the American, with an abundance of electric coffee pots, radios, vacuum cleaners, hair dryers, cameras, pocket calculators, and the like. Most Swedish households in the lower middle class have an automobile but seldom do Swedes have more than one (Sweden has two-thirds as many autos per capita as the United States).

There are many compensations in Sweden for the relative lack of private possessions and private living space. Living space there is used more efficiently, caused in part by the superior interior design of residential units. The quality of home furnishings of the average worker, in both functional and aesthetic terms, appears to be extremely high in Sweden. In addition, public services make up for some of the services lacking in the private environment. The Swede does not need a second car because of the widespread availability of excellent public transportation (40 percent of urban travel is by mass transit, compared to about 5 percent in the United States). A private yard is not necessary because of nearby excellent parks and playgrounds. Private laundry facilities are not essential due to the availability of common laundry and ironing rooms in most apartment buildings. And most Swedes live in environments where there is a relative abundance of shops, laundromats, and many other kinds of locally accessible services.

In addition, the Swede is much more likely to have what is still a dream for many Americans—a second home. One out of four Swedes either owns or has access to a summer home, and the figure is higher for those living in urban areas. Typically the long (six-week) summer vacation is spent at the summer cottage, and also many weekends throughout the year. It is not uncommon for Swedes to make a greater emotional investment in their summer home than they do in their urban apartment.

In its basic social dimensions, the life-style of the typical Swedish metropolitan male adult is not very different from his U.S. counterpart's, however much their respective residential environments may differ. The Swedish male leads a comfortable, home-centered life; in addition to his job his time is spent mainly with his immediate family and close relatives, and in informal socializing with friends. He is active in perhaps one outside organization, has no strong interest in politics, and looks on his job more as a source of income than as a career.[4] This is not the picture one has of middle-class urban apartment dwellers in the United States, who seem to have a more cosmopolitan outlook, but it is comparable with the American suburban middle mass.

In daily routine, the typical Swedish male adult does differ somewhat from his American counterpart, but he is not very different from working people in other Northern European societies. He gets up early, about 6:30 or 7:00, eats a light breakfast of coffee and a roll in the kitchen, and catches public transportation or drives a short distance to his work. After an eight-hour day, he comes home to spend a quiet evening with his family (only 6 percent of all Swedes hold a second job). On the way home from work either he or his wife will stop off at the market for food (food shopping is a more frequent activity in Sweden than in the United States). After dinner, in nice weather, he may take a walk around his neighborhood; he regularly reads one or more newspapers (the average Swedish household reads 1.5 newspapers per day, the highest rate in the world). He watches television for no more than an hour or two each evening (much less than the average American adult) and goes to bed early, about 10:00 or 11:00.

In structure, the Swedish family differs from the American in two important respects. First, due to the very low Swedish birth rate, the family is smaller, containing fewer than two children (1.7) compared to the American family's 2.3. The birth rate in Sweden is currently 11 live births per year per 1,000 population, compared to 16 in the United States; but the Swedish birth rate has been very low since the middle of the 1920s, while it is only recently that the United States birth rate has dropped to such a low level. Swedish wives born during the 1930s had about 2.2 or 2.3 children by the time they completed their childbearing years, an especially small number when compared to the 3.3 children of their counterparts in the United States.[5] In addition, the post–World War II baby boom was not felt as strongly in Sweden as in the United States. One major effect of the smaller family size in Sweden is that accommodation to the limited space of an apartment is a lesser problem than Americans might suppose.

Second, the Swedish woman is more likely to hold a job outside the home. About 80 percent of Swedish married women are gainfully employed, although more than 50 percent of these work only part time. In comparison, about 50 percent of American married women hold paying jobs, a majority of which are held part time. The metropolitan environment in Sweden offers many advantages to the working woman that are not found in the United States, including good public transportation, better child-care facilities, and low-maintenance housing.[6] These advantages tend to make the life of the working woman less harried than it appears to be in the United States. In their dual roles, employed Swedish women who are also homemakers and mothers seem not as conflict-ridden as their U.S. counterparts, although cross-national comparisons of this kind are necessarily subjective.[7]

Also, the life-styles of Swedish women who have children seem not to be as different from their childless fellow citizens as is the case in the United States. Single Swedes and childless couples naturally are less home and family oriented than the Swedes who have children. The time that others spend in child care typically is devoted to an increase in such outside-the-home activities as sports and hobby clubs, study circles, and leisure-time pursuits such as walking, bicycling, and (in warmer months) boating. Yet the childless and those with children have similar housing accommodations and share the same residential environment, and the widespread public services and facilities for children greatly lessen the time burdens on parents.

Although hard data are not available to provide empirical support, most foreign observers and Swedish commentators as well have noted that Swedes have a natural reserve and shyness that tend to inhibit them in social gatherings; it is not so easy for them as it is for Americans to mingle with strangers.[8] In part this reserve may stem from a cultural homogeneity and isolation, centuries of an absence of strangers in their midst. But the Swedish reserve goes even deeper than that of adjacent Scandinavian countries that have been similarly isolated. It makes itself felt especially in the very low level of neighboring to be found in Swedish metropolitan areas. The effects on neighboring of the Swedish personality reserve is compounded by apartment-house living in a situation of social-class heterogeneity (Swedish apartment buildings typically have a substantially higher mix of income groups than is the case of the United States, mainly due to Swedish government housing subsidies[9]). Both apartment-house living and class mixing tend to inhibit neighboring.[10] The social result of this combination of circumstances is neighborly relations that rank among the weakest in the world, contrasting strongly with the relative strength of neighborly relations in the United States and Britain.

Another striking contrast with U.S. metropolitan life-styles is the absence of religious sentiment and religious activities in Sweden.[11] Sweden may be the world's most secular nation, probably even more secular than any communist society. In metropolitan areas less than 5 percent of the population are regular church attenders, and religious thought and feeling are seldom invoked in the normal course of life the way they are in the United States. The absence of religiosity means that Swedes lack a very important form of social participation that is widely available to Americans, something that is a major component of the American local community. The lack is partially compensated for, however, by an abundance of voluntary activities, ranging from study circles to sports clubs, that are sponsored by work organizations, political parties, and the government.

Even though the life of the average Swede takes place in a comparatively urbane setting—one with small specialty shops, high-density housing, public transportation, and public parks and meeting places—the Swedish lifestyle could hardly be called urbane in the continental sense. People in Sweden do not linger long in public places; there are very few bistros, outdoor restaurants, or bars where strangers may collect for informal interaction and discussion of the day's events. The Swedish metropolitan area is designed not for ease of interpersonal contact but for ease of movement: Swedes go efficiently to work, and when the workday ends they go efficiently home, stopping only perhaps for the evening's food. Nor are the evening hours filled with the cosmopolitan pursuits that a dense urban setting makes possible. Much like the suburban American, Swedes stay close to home. Their main venture away from home base is to the summer house, where again, save for the time spent afloat on whatever body of water is nearby, life is quite homebound.

For the bourgeois family that values order, efficiency, cleanliness, and a high standard of public services, there is probably no better metropolitan environment than that of a major Swedish urban area. Everything is in its place, everything works, and everything is clean. Yet the great material affluence of the American private milieu is absent, and the vitality and street life of continental cities is not to be found. The life of a Swede is characterized by a high degree of organization and efficiency, but also by a real sense of privacy and impersonality. It is not only the climate that is meant when foreigners suggest that Sweden lacks warmth.

### The United States: Private Affluence amidst Public Squalor

The characteristic middle-class metropolitan American lives in a single-family detached house[12] in a low-density suburb. By international standards the home is extremely spacious,[13] and the residents have a large amount of private space. In addition to internal space, the family has substantial outside yard space, often enclosed with a fence or shrubbery. Especially in the warmer climates, the yard becomes a true extension of the interior living space, with many activities taking place there that might otherwise take place within the home. The home is well furnished, with a great many labor-saving appliances, more than are found in the homes of any other country. These include dishwashers, washers and dryers, garbage disposal units, and freezers.

Many homes have a special room for television viewing and other recreational activities. Recreational equipment is also frequently found in the backyard. And often the garage has been fixed up to be a man's workshop. It is quite common for garages to be converted into living space, with the cars parked outside or under an open carport.

The house ordinarily is located in an all-residential district, one from which commercial and industrial uses have been excluded. Save for neighboring families, therefore, few facilities and services are within walking distance. Indeed, many suburban communities fail to construct sidewalks, believing that the amount of potential use does not warrant the cost. There being scant public transportation, usually consisting only of occasional bus service, getting to work, to shopping, and to leisure-time pursuits is done almost entirely by automobile. Fortunately, many American middle-class families have two cars, yet this often is not enough, especially if both parents work and there are teenagers in the family.

Shopping is typically done once or twice a week at a large supermarket, with occasional shopping at automobile-oriented convenience markets. Not commonly found in the other societies is the large, automobile-oriented retail mall, a shopping precinct that has largely replaced "downtown." Work may be at a nearby industrial park, a commercial center, or at some outlying workplace. Work, shopping, and residence tend to be geographically separated to a larger degree than elsewhere, with each destination requiring a separate auto trip.

It can reasonably be said that, relative to people in the other three countries, Americans live in an environment of private affluence and public squalor. The American household is somewhat larger than those of the other societies, averaging 2.75 persons per unit, and the extra dwelling space that Americans possess is in part a natural outcome of this fact. But the large amount of space stems also from Americans' very high standard of private consumption, a standard that in part represents a trade-off with public services. While Europeans are taxed at a significantly higher rate than Americans,[14] with a large portion of the monies thus raised used to support community facilities and services, Americans are spending these "saved taxes" on private consumption. The amount of material goods possessed by the American, for example, because of having more disposable income, far exceeds those of the Swede or Englishman at a comparable income level. This consumption of material goods, in its turn, requires additional private space for use, display, and storage.

The environmental squalor of American metropolitan communities stems in part from their dispersed character and the associated dominance of the automobile. But the relative lack of public funding dooms public services of all kinds—parks and playgrounds, public housing, public transportation—to a level of quality that is meager at best by European standards. The poor quality of older communities, for example the inner-city slums in most older American cities of even modest size, also results from the lack of publicly financed planning efforts to direct urban growth and renew town centers. The American metropolitan scene is also blemished in European eyes by the commercialization of the landscape through billboards, strip commercial development, and the absence of aesthetic controls.

Most Americans appear not to be unhappy about this trade-off of public services for private consumption. In their spacious homes and oversized cars they have a strong sense, as individuals and as family units, of being the material kings of the world. Moreover, higher taxes are one of the most politically anathematic issues in the nation, indicating that the trade-off has a strong political blessing.

The typical working American arises about 7:00 to 7:30, eats a large breakfast by European standards, and drives to work, arriving there by 8:30 or 9:00.[15] The working day is eight hours, a period that is now usual in almost all advanced societies. But due to commuting, the American tends to be away from home longer than workers in the other countries. Much more than in the other countries, food shopping is done in bulk. The large capacity of American refrigerators and the widespread ownership of home freezers accentuates this tendency.

The American is not a great reader of books and newspapers, but is the world's most avid television viewer, averaging about twenty-two hours per week.[16] For many Americans television viewing is the main evening diversion, although a night out at the movies is also popular, especially among younger people and on weekends. The American seldom walks for pleasure and bicycles only very infrequently, but driving for pleasure is not uncommon, especially on weekends.

More than is the case with people in the other countries, the American informally neighbors, a phenomenon especially common among home-owners (64 percent of all American housing units are owned) and among families with children. Neighboring may involve the provision of service and aid (for example in connection with home maintenance and child care), cooperative work efforts, and informal socializing in one another's homes, the latter being especially common for women.

Just as distinctively American is the pattern of church attendance and church activities. Nearly half of metropolitan Americans are actively involved in church affairs, something that provides a significant focus for their lives in a social as well as religious way. Church activities are one of the few things in American life in which all ages, and all members of a family, may be involved.

Another distinctive American life-style characteristic is the second job. Moonlighting is common in metropolitan areas, especially among men, and is one reason that the United States appears from the perspective of the other countries to be a nation of workaholics. Americans do work more hours each day than do Swedes and the English, and they also have much shorter summer vacations, averaging only two or three weeks.

Other than in church activities, Americans participate in "community affairs" about on a par with the other nations. Volunteerism and voluntary organizations are a pronounced part of the American scene and are especially important in the lives of women who are not gainfully employed. The voluntary sector, for example, plays a role in social welfare services not found in the other countries, where public agencies and their paid employees typically replace the volunteer worker. Politically, Americans seem no more involved than Swedes or the English; certainly, their attendance at the polls on election day is much less frequent than that of voters in the other countries. In adult education activities, the three countries appear to be on a par.

Because of the large size of their homes, together with widespread home ownership, Americans dote on their houses more than the Europeans. They probably lead the world in the time and money spent on maintenance and improvement, activities that in an age of inflation tend more and more to be done by the homeowner rather than outsiders. Especially for men, upkeep and upgrading are outlets that partly offset the passivity of the hours before the tube. In addition, where and when the climate is favorable, many Americans are avid gardeners, although in this regard they come in a distant second to the English.

Finally, one must note the Americans' mobility as well as instability. Americans change their place of residence at a rate about twice that of the Europeans. There is some evidence that the American mobility rate is not increasing; in fact it has probably leveled off. And two-thirds of the moves are within the same county. Nevertheless, the rate at which Americans uproot themselves in search of better housing, of different-size housing, and of jobs is almost certainly the highest in the West. The effect this may have on community life is a topic taken up in the following chapters.

At least as compared with life in European societies (and Japan), American life is also marked by a high degree of economic insecurity. American society has the character of a gambler's society: You may hit the jackpot and become really rich (something that is extremely difficult today, for example, in Sweden), but you can also with relative ease find yourself "out in the street." American employment policies are much less geared to job stability than are European policies. Many health costs require private payments to the extent that a serious medical problem can be financially disastrous to the individual. And the pressures for ever-expanding personal consumption can quickly lead to indebtedness and even bankruptcy, to cite but a few examples.[17]

The difference between the well-off American and the person not so well off can be very great indeed. It has been estimated that Americans in the top–5 percent income bracket earn thirteen times as much as those in the bottom 5 percent. Comparable figures for Britain are six times as much, and for Sweden only three times as much.[18] But the differences among the countries are not only in private incomes but in community support. The American poor are able to rely on community support to a much lower degree than their European counterparts.

Thus to be reasonably well off in the United States with job stability and economic security in old age, is to have a life of great personal freedom and affluence. But to be poor, or even economically marginal, is to be a second-class citizen in a way that is not found to be acceptable by the English or Swedish societies.

### England: Social Comfort in Aging, Urban Villages

The typical middle-class domicile in England is the semidetached or terraced house (called a row house in the United States) on a narrow street in a built-up area next to a major center of population.[19] The house is quite spacious by European standards, but the facilities within it are much more limited in number and primitive in quality than are those of Sweden or the United States. Kitchen equipment is relatively old-fashioned, refrigerators are small, freezers are rare. It is common for the British family, therefore, to shop for food more often than the American family. (The difficulties of frequent shopping are mitigated to some extent by daily milk delivery, Britain being the only modern society that still extensively maintains this home service.)

The house typically is on a street from which nonresidential uses have been excluded, but shopping districts consisting of a multitude of small shops are often in the immediate vicinity. Due to the relatively high densities the districts tend to be within walking distance, and groceries may be carried home by hand (although in-town supermarkets and bulk shopping are on the increase.) Public transportation in the form of bus service is much more readily available than in the United States, however, and people generally use it to get to work as well as for major shopping trips. Most middle-class residents own one (but seldom more than one) car, which is used less frequently than the American car; it is especially important for weekend trips. The car is often parked on the street or in the front yard in a carport.

British residential areas often have much more of a village appearance than do those of either Sweden or the United States, because of the densities, the narrow streets, a relatively active street life, and an old-fashioned appearance. The life-style of the English metropolitan dweller follows suit—it is in some respects like the life-style of people in a small village. (This is certainly a life-style that many of the English romantically idealize.) People live very close to one another, yet they have outdoor areas where they mingle. At least four types of specialty shops are often visited during the course of a week: one for meats, one for bakery goods, one for vegetables (the green grocer), and one for dry goods. Together with the low level of automobile ownership, this shopping pattern gives many English suburbs a bustling street life, a kind of village friendliness.

The English are quite home centered, and unlike the Swedes and a few Americans they have only one home on which to lavish their attention. Among the world's finest gardeners, they attend the backyard garden particulary well. In interior furnishings, the English home could be described as cozy rather than attractive. Many foreigners judge the decor to be well below that of the American home and, especially, that of the Swedish home. Part of the problem is the relatively low material level of many English homes, which among other things is manifest in what is apparent undermaintenance. One seldom finds the bright and shiny look so characteristic of Swedish, and to a slightly lesser extent American, interiors.

The English adult male goes to work by car or bus at a relatively late hour by continental standards, and returns home relatively early. The workday is not quite as long as it is in the other countries, and very few English people hold second jobs. Somewhat fewer women work outside the home than in Sweden or the United States,[20]and certainly compared to Sweden the English housewife, or "mum," appears to hold a rather honored position.

English leisure time is spent in front of the television set or at the cinema, or reading a newspaper or book. Radio is considerably better developed and utilized in England than it is in the United States. While there is a certain ease of contact with neighbors, there is relatively little formal entertaining in England (and what there is is mainly a middle-class activity). Much social life revolves around informal contact with close family and relatives. In nice weather, the English people may be found tramping in the country, which is never far away. Or they may go country driving in the automobile. Although not quite to the same low degree as Sweden, religious activities are quite weak in England, and are primarily the province of women. Local cultural life in England still contains considerable vitality, however, with community-based theatre and concert groups being particularly in evidence.[21]

The unique English institution is the pub, or public house. During the lunch and dinner hours, it is a principal place of life and informal contact for both the middle and working classes, particularly for men. Although pubs close down for several hours in the middle of the afternoon, it is common to find them so busy about 2:00 or 2:30 that one may even wonder how the serious work of England actually gets done!

Most Englishmen have their favorite local pub, and visit it with regularity. For many English people, indeed, the pub is almost an extension of their living rooms. A warm and open place, where anyone may strike up a conversation with a stranger, there is an air of conviviality there that is totally foreign to Sweden. The same atmosphere can be found in some working-class taverns in the United States, but in Britain pubs are a main habitat as well for persons well up into the upper middle class. Each social class tends to have its own pub, however, so it is not a place for class mixing. The division of a single pub into two sections, "saloon" and "bar," can also reflect social-class distinctions.

The summer vacation in England is only about two weeks, and thus comparable to the American vacation, but an additional week often is taken during another part of the year. The English have become among the world's great travelers, and trips abroad, especially in recent years through the vehicle of the charter flight, are now almost as prevalent as they are in Sweden. More common still is to rent for the vacation period a cottage in the country or a caravan at the seaside, each a location where the English family feels it is a respectable distance from the cares of civilization.

What may characterize the English life-style more than anything else is the term *comfortable*. It is not material comfort so much, for homes are cold and drafty and appliances are few, but social comfort. The life-style is comfortable like an old shoe: it may not look so nice on the outside, but it feels great and has the right fit. The English have worked out a life-style that provides them with a great deal of leisure, an unhurried round of activity, and environments, like pubs and neighborhoods, that seldom change.

The comfortable feel of life is also based on a relative inflexibility of social roles. Women in England seem to accept "old-fashioned" roles more readily than do women in Sweden or the United States, and even relations among the classes are subject to strong and relatively inflexible patterning. This inflexibility of roles is not without problems, as most modern commentators point out, but it does lead to an unstressful social atmosphere and a predictability of life not found to the same degree in the other nations. The English give to outsiders signals that there is really no need to change traditional patterns, which, after all, were looked up to by the rest of the world a century ago as the very epitome of civilization.

English life is further enhanced by the inherent decency, civility, and friendliness of the English people. The English are relatively open, at least by Swedish standards, and are at the same time almost unfailingly courteous. This polite friendliness can readily be seen in the interaction between clerks and customers in the neighborhood shops, and on the part of bus drivers, milk deliverers, and the police, who manage to be gracious under even the most trying of circumstances—something that makes England a very pleasant place to visit. One also finds a formality and personal reserve in England that set it apart from the United States. There are fewer glad-handers, social oilers, and fast-talking, aggressive people, types that are often commented upon by the English who visit their metropolitan "American cousins."

When all is said, however, the English urban residential environment is antiquated and deteriorating, inefficient and subject to frequent breakdown, and at least questionable on aesthetic grounds. It may have a comfortable feel to the English, but a journey from metropolitan England to metropolitan Sweden points up that in some respects England does not appear to have entered the modern age. Unless the English are immune from material envy, it seems only a matter of time before their contentedness turns to bitterness and feelings of national inferiority. Within the last few years, in fact, such attitudes have definitely been on the upswing.[22]

### Summary of Metropolitan Life Styles in Advanced Societies

A comparison of life-styles in the three metropolitan settings points up many qualities that vary with the characteristic metropolitan form of each nation. The Swedish apartment–public transportation complex, the American detached house-automobile milieu, and the English urban village all shape life-styles in the expected ways. It is important to emphasize that the effects of differing characteristics of the residential environment are accentuated in the lives of those who have limited territorial mobility. Women more than men, children more than adults, and the poor more than the rich are rooted in their locales, being less able to move beyond them. This is demonstrated through the special advantages that women, especially working women, gain from the high quality of the Swedish metropolitan environment. Typically provided with many facilities and services that are important to their life-style, they are environmentally quite favored compared to their American counterparts. This is even more true if the comparison is between relatively poor working women with children.

The "public face" of the metropolitan settings can also be seen to have sharp consequences for private lives. The United States, with its public squalor, in a sense forces people to retreat into their private domains and to make those domains as spacious, attractive, and comfortable as possible (which in turn is enabled by the high level of private disposable income). Sweden, with its great metropolitanwide order, efficiency, and attractiveness, presents its dwellers with far fewer public hassles, yet has not at the same time been able to achieve conditions that draw people out of their private realms and provide them with communal ties.

Of course purely social characteristics in each society also shape lifestyles in significant ways. Organized religion in the United States provides many with a semicommunal tie of a type that is largely absent in Sweden and England. In Sweden, the social pattern of ownership of second homes helps to ameliorate the anonymity of urban life for many, and the relatively low level of neighboring in urban areas is generated not only by high-density apartment living but also by aspects of the Swedish character. And what one could call the social drinking pattern in England, centered around the neighborhood pub, gives typical life-styles in that society a special and unique attribute.

Yet despite the many differences that distinguish the metropolitan lifestyles of these three societies, a number of very important commonalities can also be discerned. Each of the residential settings we have examined is, after all, highly metropolitan in character, and from a more lofty vantage point the life-styles associated with each setting bear substantial similarities. The similarities suggest that there exist in all advanced, metropolitan societies social forces or trends whose influence tends to override the effects of political, economic, social, and physical differences.

To begin, it bears repeating that the main social unit in metropolitan areas is the small household—typically consisting of several interrelated family members but increasingly made up of singles or several unrelated individuals. A larger network of relatives and friends exists, but at some distance from each household (less so in the case of England). Rather than being the center for a network of activities, the household is better characterized as a home base, a place from which one goes out and to which one returns. With work often at great distance, and social networks widespread, the household becomes less a center of life and more a retreat or refuge to which one withdraws from public activities into private pleasures.[23]

Most adult family members in each nation still are strongly familistic in life-style, however. Their lives center on home and family and are organized in terms of family values; they maintain close ties with parents and other relatives.[24] A *career* orientation, sometimes regarded as an alternative to familism, is not strong (in these, and probably all other societies), the job being mainly a means to a satisfying home life. With their interests centered on their own family activities and leisure-time pursuits, most adults are not active in local politics and community affairs.

Nor are the metropolitan adults in these nations oriented strongly toward an urban culture; they show little concern for the arts, fine restaurants, and urban intellectual life. Although their environmental settings are urban, with the Swedes especially having close physical ties to the city, these metropolitan dwellers have social, cultural, and environmental preferences that direct them away from the city rather than toward it. If they were to move, it would be further from the city, not closer to it; they seek the countryside for vacation and leisure, and many hope to retire to smaller places. Thus most of the metropolitan residents in each nation could be characterized as rural and small-town dwellers at heart who live near a city for economic reasons: jobs, commercial facilities, and such social services as health and education.

This familistic, nonurban life-style may be in part a vestige of the rural and small-town roots that many metropolitan dwellers in each nation have. It is likely that only a minority of the metropolitan adults are native to urban areas. The role played by nonurban background and upbringing is highlighted by the changing life-styles of today's metropolitan-bred young adults, who tend to be much less familistic than their parents.

The urban-living singles typically have a life-style that has been called *consumership*—an emphasis on making enough money to have a good time and to enjoy life through material consumption. Persons having this life-style are not familistic, especially in the sense of child-centeredness, nor are their lives devoted to the pursuit of a career (a life-style found mainly among members of the upper middle class). Young consumers are more urban oriented than their familistic counterparts, but they also tend generally to be oriented away from the city, to the leisure and recreation associated with the countryside. As do others, they live near the city for jobs, services, and the higher standard of living that such a location brings.

The daily lives of metropolitan dwellers are highly structured and time oriented, a structure that does not vary by season. Most adults arise, get to work, and arrive home at a fixed time each day. In this sense their lives are orderly and highly predictable.

The geographic separation of home and work has its counterpart in a strongly felt cultural and emotional separation. The job increasingly is something that one does, must do, during certain hours each week so as to permit a rich and rewarding private life. Once the workday ends, and one retires to the household refuge, the attempt is deliberately made to leave the cares of the work world entirely behind. People thus come to segment their lives strongly into the world of work, where somebody else is boss and they do what they are told, and the world at home, where they do what they want and are their own boss.

Thus the following overall portrayal can be sketched of metropolitan life-styles, drawing from the common experiences of the three nations. People's lives center on a household, a very small group of intimates who share a separate domicile. The group exists in an environment—both the local neighborhood and the metropolitan area as a whole—that is felt to be rather alien. (This is less the case in England than in the other countries.) That is, most household members would rather live in a smaller and more personally accessible environment. They venture into this environment on a daily basis, mainly to earn the money necessary to support their seemingly more rewarding private lives in which they have the personal freedoms and pleasures often missing in the work environment. Public and private lives become highly distinct, with the development of different modes of thought and even behavior appropriate to each.

At the same time that the household becomes more privatized and cut off from the outside world, its own social structure seems to be gaining a kind of internal privatization, one in which social involvement and inti-macy are on the decline. Television has clearly increased the amount of time people spend in the privacy of their homes, for example, but televi-sion viewing does not involve much social interaction. Moreover, as the number of people in each household continues to decline, television view-ing itself takes place in the presence of increasingly fewer persons.

The privacy and separateness of the household world are muted to some degree by external social networks of friends and relatives, by some neigh-boring (especially through the church in the United States), by some work-connected "after-hours" social activities (especially in Sweden), and by pubs in Britain. But in each nation a trend toward the privatization of life is a major identifiable commonality that conceptually links the citizens of societies whose urban environments are so different but whose societal macrostructures are so similar. The metropolitan environment itself is not seen for the most part as a human community, one to which a person can intimately relate and have feelings of identity and belonging. It is less a community than an arena within which life takes place, a bundle of necessary facilities and services that economically binds an individual but about which one feels at best affectively neutral. It is to the nature of the metropolitan community that we now turn.

## Notes

1. Saul D. Feldman and Gerald W. Thielbar, *Life Styles: Diversity in American Society*, 2d ed. (Boston: Little, Brown, 1975).
2. William Michelson, *Man and His Urban Environment* (Reading, MA: Addison-Wesley, 1976), ch. 3.
3. Data from mid-1970s. Most Swedish data in this chapter are from the Swedish Information Service. U.S. data are from the U.S. Census.
4. This portrait is from my book *The Suburban Environment: Sweden and the United States* (Chicago: University of Chicago Press, 1977). See also Marvin E. Olsen, "Interest Association Participation and Political Activity in the United States and Sweden," *Journal of Voluntary Action Research* 17 (Fall 1974).
5. Richard F. Tomasson, *Sweden: Prototype of Modern Society* (New York: Random House, 1970), p. 188.
6. These advantages are explored in Popenoe, *Suburban Environment*.
7. See G.R. Wekerle, R. Peterson, and D. Morley, eds., *New Space for Women* (Boulder, Co.: Westview, 1980); Tomasson, *Sweden*, ch. 6; and Birgitta Linner, "What Does Equality Between the Sexes Imply?" *American Journal of Orthopsychiatry* 41 (October 1971).
8. Paul B. Austin, *On Being Swedish* (Coral Gables: University of Miami Press, 1968).
9. Bruce Headey, *Housing Policy in the Developed Economy* (New York: St. Martin's Press, 1978).
10. Suzanne Keller, *The Urban Neighborhood* (New York: Random House, 1968).
11. Tomasson, *Sweden*, ch. 3.
12. This house type made up 62 percent of all American housing in 1980.
13. Among advanced nations the United States has the lowest percentage of two-room houses (2 percent), and is second only to Canada in highest percentage of houses having seven rooms or more (21 percent). Average persons per room in the United States is .5; in the United Kingdon, .6; and in Sweden, .7. *Social Indicators III* (Washington, DC: Bureau of the Census, 1980), p. 154.
14. Tax revenue as percentage of 1972 GNP was United States, 27.8 percent; Great Britain, 37.7 percent; and Sweden, 41.8 percent. Arnold J. Heidenheimer, Hugh Heclo, and Carolyn Teich Adams, *Comparative Public Policy* (New York: St. Martin's Press, 1975), p. 228.
15. For time-use data comparing European countries with the United States (although neither Sweden nor Britain is represented), see Alexander Szalai, Philip Converse, Pierre Feldheim, Erwin Scheuch, and Philip Stone, *The Use of Time*

(The Hague: Mouton, 1972). For American data, see John P. Robinson, *How Americans Use Their Time* (New York: Praeger, 1977); and R.A. Berk and S.F. Berk, *Labor and Leisure at Home* (Beverly Hills: Sage, 1979).

16. *Social Indicators III*, p. 561.
17. For comparative evaluations of economic welfare, see Heidenheimer et al., *Comparative Public Policy*; Harold J. Wilensky, *The Welfare State and Equality* (Berkeley: University of California Press, 1975); and Alfred J. Kahn and S.B. Kamerman, *Not for the Poor Alone* (New York: Harper & Row, 1975).
18. E.O. Wright, *Class Structure and Income Determination* (New York: Academic Press, 1979), p. 232.
19. Useful introductions to contemporary British life are: Judith Ryder and H. Silver, *Modern English Society* (London: Methuen, 1970); Trevor Noble, *Modern Britain: Structure and Change* (London: Batsford, 1975); John Irwin, *Modern Britain* (London: Allen & Unwin, 1976); R.E. Pahl, *Patterns of Urban Life* (New York: Humanities Press, 1970); and Daniel Snowman, *Britain and America* (New York: Harper, 1977).
20. The percentage is increasing very rapidly, however, and is now nearly up to the U.S. level.
21. See Snowman, *Britain and America*.
22. An excellent discussion of this is Jane Kramer, "A Reporter in Europe," *New Yorker*, May 11, 1981. See also Ralf Dahrendorf, *On Britain* (Chicago: University of Chicago Press, 1982).
23. The bifurcation of life activities into public and private worlds is explored in P. Berger, B. Berger, and H. Kellner, *The Homeless Mind* (New York: Random House, 1973).
24. The life-style categories of familism, career, and consumership were originally developed by Wendell Bell. See Bell, "The City, the Surburb, and a Theory of Social Choice," in *The New Urbanization*, ed. Scott Greer et al. (New York: St. Martin's Press, 1968), ch. 7.

# 6

# The Structure of the Metropolitan Community

In the age of mass society it is common intellectually to disparage the importance of the "local community," emphasizing instead the extralocal forces and trends that dominate our lives: war and peace, the national economy and political order, and mass culture, to cite some major examples.[1] It does not make much difference, the proposition goes, whether you live in Chicago, Los Angeles, or Atlanta, life is about the same (assuming a material standard of living comparability): same inflation, television programs, fast food joints, and freeways. This proposition is hard to deny. Although there are significant interregional differences within the United States, one's life does not change very much in a move from one metropolitan area to another.

Without any doubt the metropolitan community is to a large extent a product and even a captive social creature of the larger social systems of region, state, nation, and world.[2] Metropolitan areas without exception exist in centralized societies in which political, economic, and social interdependencies extend well beyond the metropolitan boundaries, and in which control, especially political and economic control, rests in large part elsewhere. Thus the agglomeration of people brought together in a metropolitan area is itself but a piece of larger political and economic systems. And the political and economic autonomy of metropolitan citizens is relatively limited; what happens in the larger systems is often of greater importance to them than what takes place locally.

But at least cross-nationally, as we have examined in earlier chapters, metropolitan areas do show some significant differences that have real human impact. Moreover, the metropolitan community has a certain internal structure that, however much it may be the product of larger social forces, is clearly quite distinct from the structure of community types that preceded the metropolis historically, and that still exist today in much of

93

the world. In switching from one metropolitan area to another, Americans do not escape the web of this historically unique community configuration. It is to an exploration of the internal structure of the metropolitan community, both as a particular community type and one with cross-national variations, that this chapter is devoted.

To begin, a brief theoretical excursus is necessary to define some key terms that will be used. The social structure of a local community of any kind refers to what holds the community members together in one place, the linkages or bonds that enable them successfully to remain interdependent upon one another, and that permit the community as a whole to function. The bonds that hold communities together are of three main types: functional, political, and social.[3] The functional bond, formally defined, is "the facilitative or complementary effect of one activity or social process on the operation of other processes within the same system."[4] Functional bonds generate what is called functional integration, and the kind of social relationship most typical of the functional bond is the exchange relationship: people acting toward others in order to receive a reward or return of some kind. The common community arenas of the functional bond are the marketplace and the work organization. Without the functional bond—the exchange of goods and services among people—there would be little reason for a community to exist at all. Within the social sciences the functional bond and functional integration are the primary concerns of the discipline of economics; they can be measured in such terms as labor markets, consumer trading networks, and dominance and subdominance among interrelated economic systems.

The political bond may be defined as "the conscious attempt to create or regularize the practical interconnections of activities."[5] Through this bond the people in a community seek to rise above the exigencies of the market to achieve the collective goals of the system, goals that often involve modifying in some way the "free" operation of the market. Political bonds generate what is called political integration, and the typical kind of social relationship related to the political bond is the legal-bureaucratic relationship: people acting toward one another in terms of accepted legal or bureaucratic rules. Coercion and conflict also are commonly involved, however. The community arenas of the political bond and political integration are those involving public, collective decision making in a hierarchy of power and authority, especially the local government.

The third main community bond is the social. This bond is also referred to by some as the consensual bond, or the bond of solidarity, and in contrast to each of the others it takes heavily symbolic and subjective forms. The bonds of consensus or solidarity can range from what can be called the positive mutual reinforcement of community activities and community life, with a strong element of cooperative social relationships, to the much weaker mutual noninterference, the situation of live and let live. Of course the social bond also can be virtually absent, with the political and economic life of the community characterized by open conflict. Social bonds generate social integration, and a community is said to rank high in social integration "to the extent that specialized participants perceive, positively evaluate and identify with the network of interrelated activities."[6]

These three bonds, then, provide the bases for a community's social structure. The functional bond is typically the basis of the community's being together in the first place; the political bond expresses the community's capacity for collective action; and the social bond denotes the cooperative and symbolically solidary nature of community relationships. The classic small and isolated community in a weak national society ranks close to the top in the strength and congruence of its functional, political, and social bonds: the community members work and trade together, take collective action when necessary, and feel a strong cooperative spirit toward one another. The question is, how does the metropolitan community appear in these terms?

## The Metropolitan Community

The metropolitan community as a whole is to a much larger degree an economic rather than a political or social unit. The community's most fundamental feature is that of being a single labor market: within the metropolitan area workers compete with one another for jobs, and the geographic size of the area is very much determined by the length of the journey to work. Once jobs are located, people live at a distance from those jobs that is fixed by daily travel times, typically not exceeding a maximum of about one hour each way. As metropolitan areas grow in size so that this rough one-hour barrier becomes abrogated, it is common for centrally located employment points to move to the periphery; thus jobs to some extent follow people as well as the reverse.

Whatever unity a metropolitan area may express in economic terms typically is not paralleled politically, especially in the United States. While the boundaries of economic systems are readily expandable, the boundaries of political systems are more enduring and sometimes even inviolate. The political organization of people becomes fixed within certain jurisdictions that become exceedingly difficult to modify, with any change seeming to strike at fundamental rights and privileges that most people enjoy, as well as at political power arrangements that are not willingly relinquished. As the metropolitan economic system expands, it overrides smaller-scale governmental units whose boundaries were established to encompass earlier and smaller economic aggregations. Notably in the United States, the number of these smaller units can be bewildering, consisting of boroughs and townships, towns and cities, and counties, making up a hugh patchwork quilt of governmental forms. It must also be noted that even when new political units are developed to coincide with changing economic realities, the new units themselves can quickly become outmoded due to further metropolitan expansion. This problem of mismatch between economics and politics is felt in each of the three advanced societies, although Sweden and England have come much further in resolving it than has the United States, as will be discussed below.

Because the establishment of governmental boundaries around the new metropolitan economic system is so difficult, collective decision making by and for metropolitan areas becomes in some cases almost impossible, and public decision making takes the form either of action by higher-level government units (in the United States, the state and federal governments) or by political bargaining among the constituent governmental units within the metropolis.[7] The latter mode of political decision making can often have one-sided results, with the rich and powerful districts of the metropolis quickly getting the upper hand.

The social basis of the metropolitan community is even more problematic than the political basis. The social solidarity of any community of people, as James Coleman has pointed out, can be based on four social situations.[8] First, people can feel a sense of oneness because it is traditional and expected that they do so, a situation that is quite foreign to the metropolitan scene. Second, social solidarity can be based on the bonds of mutual understanding that follow from participation in common work activities. This basis can be seen clearly in the classic rural village, and even in the small industrial town, but it is not the situation characteristic of metropolitan areas. Third, social solidarity can flow from the realization by a group of people that, although they are engaged in different activities, they are striving for similar objectives, and the achievement of these objectives requires a unity of feeling and purpose. In metropolitan areas this basis of solidarity exists weakly around such economic issues as industrial growth. (And in a certain sense it could be said to exist around such weak issues as the success of sport teams.) The sense of striving for similar objectives is considerably more significant as a basis of social solidarity in England and Sweden than it is in the United States.

Fourth, social solidarity can be built around the common dependence of community activities on the same events: crime, fire, nuclear attack, economic recession, transportation breakdown, for a few examples. Through being subject to the consequences of such events, people gain a feeling that they are "in the same boat together." While this basis, also, may be only weakly manifest in most metropolitan areas, it is the main basis upon which many political leaders rely when they seek to promote greater metropolitan solidarity.

We have been discussing the social structure of the metropolis as if it were a single community of people. If instead we look at the metropolis as a collection of local subcommunities, ranging in hierarchy from the local neighborhood to the region, a slightly different picture emerges. The local neighborhood within metropolitan areas is typically a social unit at best, and seldom a political or functional unit. As often as not, however, the metropolitan neighborhood is barely even a social unit; it may exist in name only, or be merely a collection of people who have little connection with one another. At the next level of the hierarchy, towns, and suburbs within metropolitan areas are typically political units, often also having reasonably intact bonds of social solidarity. But most have ceased to make sense in economic or functional terms. Finally, the metropolitan region as a whole is a functional unit, but it characteristically lacks political and social bonds.

Thus the metropolitan community poses for its residents an extremely segmented and fragmented character. Social attachments may be one place, perhaps to a neighborhood or other local area; political attachments are to a town or other governmental jurisdiction; and economic or functional attachments are to neither of these units. This fragmentation has the effect of further casting people's social, political, and functional attachments beyond the metropolitan area entirely, to nation and mass society. And it has the consequence of further insuring the loss of political, economic, and social autonomy, a loss that already is the lot of local communities in advanced societies. The corrosion of local attachments and local autonomy is further accelerated by the widespread residential mobility in these societies, a mobility which, in the United States especially, generates strong feelings of transiency and residential instability.

The increases in community scale and fragmentation, and in the residential mobility and geographic interdependence of urban citizens, must not be seen in a wholly negative light. The "breakdown of local community" involves the diminution of social parochialisms, the development of larger and much more efficient economic networks, and more centralized political control that seems necessary if not always desired. Indeed, to a degree these trends seem as necessary as they are inevitable. Nevertheless, it is very important to realize that they cast residents into an historically unusual position vis-à-vis their local communities, with daily life being affected in ways that are often unwanted and even deleterious.[9] These ways are explored in the following chapter.

### Cross-National Differences in Metropolitan Community Structure

In functional bonds, there is little to choose among the metropolitan areas of the three societies. Dominated by capitalist economies, the economic ties that internally bind the metropolitan areas of Sweden, the United States, and England are fundamentally the same: the exchanging of goods and services through the marketplace under the guiding hand of government regulation, ranging from most restrictive in Sweden to least in the United States. It is in their metropolitan political and social bonds that the three nations show some notable differences.

*Sweden*

Perhaps the outstanding characteristic of Swedish metropolitan areas, from a comparative perspective, is the degree to which they are centrally planned, with public goals consistently taking precedence over private interests. The results of this centralized planning were analyzed in earlier chapters; here we shall discuss the ways in which this planning is rooted in, and made possible by, the structure of the Swedish metropolitan community.

First, there exists in the metropolitan areas of Sweden a relatively strong political and social consensus about metropolitan issues, one that tends to override the parochial interests of particular local communities within the metropolis.[10] This consensus is based in part on the comparatively small scale of Swedish metropolitan areas, and on the homogeneity of the metropolitan population. It is enhanced by the relatively limited residential differentiation in Swedish communities.[11] The neighborhood mixing of population in terms of social class, ethnicity, and stage of the life cycle occurs to a much larger degree than in the other two nations, thus minimizing a principal basis of local neighborhood parochialism that can undermine metropolitanwide decision making.

Also, local "attachments to place" in Swedish metropolitan areas, to the degree that they exist at all, extend over large urban districts—western Stockholm, for example. The more localized and often named urban neighborhoods to which many are attached in Britain and the United States are not as common. This characteristic is reflected in the structure of political representation at the local government levels. Most urban political representation is "at large," and not rooted in wards and other local districts the way it is in the other countries.[12]

To account fully for the metropolitan consensus, one must look in addition to cultural and historical factors that lie beyond the metropolitan boundaries. Most important is the "natural" cooperativeness of Scandinavian peoples, in this case compounded by a respect for, confidence in, and even deference toward civil servants such as planners and local government administrators.[13]

Metropolitan-level decision making in Sweden is made possible not only by a strong political and social consensus, however, but also by the presence of governmental jurisdictions whose boundaries approximate the geographic spread of the metropolitan area as a functional unit. In 1968, for example, the city and county governments of Stockholm were combined into a single unit, and the resulting "regional government" has powers unlike anything found in U.S. metropolitan areas. This was but one instance of local-government consolidations that reduced the number of Swedish governmental units during the period 1950-75 from about 2,500 to a mere 278, something unheard of in the United States.[14] In many of these consolidations government jurisdictions were made to correspond much more closely with functional areas.

The combination of these cultural and historical factors, then, largely accounts for Sweden's great success in centralized metropolitan planning and development. In no other Western society have government planners been granted the amount of authority they have in Sweden, and Swedish metropolitan areas today are the closest in the Western world to fulfilling the planners' goals of order, efficiency, beauty, and social justice. Indeed, centralized planning in Sweden has been so dominant that a frequent urban political issue in recent decades has focused on trying to take planning away from the experts and bring it closer to the people. American observers, especially, tend to see in Swedish planning practice an undemocratic, elitist system in which the voice of the grass roots has been entirely too weak.[15] Some of the more unpleasant aspects of Sweden's postwar metropolitan development, for example, such as the massive highrise apartment blocks of the late 1960s and early 1970s, have been blamed on an overcentralized planning system in which the people's voice was too seldom heard.[16] Yet few outside observers would deny that, at least in traditional planning terms, Swedish metropolitan development has been a resounding success.

The same factors that account for the successful planning and development of Sweden's metropolitan areas also contribute to the "tone" of its metropolitan community life. Because it is less rooted in the parochialisms of local neighborhoods, Swedish metropolitan life as a whole is more "cosmopolitan" than that of the other countries. One does not find in Sweden anything like Gerald Suttles's "defended community," where neighbors are actively engaged in defending and protecting their territory against the encroachments, both real and symbolic, of outsiders.[17] In fact, relatively few social groupings exist that are organized around neighborhood lines, such as the community councils, property owners associations, and neighborhood-based voluntary associations of the United States and Britain. Most Swedish voluntary associations are linked to societywide organizations, government-sponsored programs, or places of work (many sports groups are linked to work organizations). Some of these associations are organized in terms of local community boundaries, but seldom are they linked to indigenous local community groups.[18] Thus the "local attachments to place" of the metropolitan Swede are quite weak, a weakness that is compounded by the high rate of rental rather than owned housing. (Property ownership almost always generates a higher sense of neighborhood attachment and protectiveness, partly owing to the financial investments that are involved.)

Weak local attachments in Sweden are related, in addition, to very low church attendance. Especially in the United States, neighborhood churches often bring together people living in a local area, and provide a bond of deep and enduring character. While the Swedish church is organized in terms of local parishes, and it has certain functions not found in the other countries, such as the collection of vital statistics, church attendance of less than 5 percent makes the church of minimal importance from a social point of view.[19]

If attachments to neighborhood are relatively weak in Sweden, are there any higher-level areal units that may capture people's need for attachment to place? While weak local attachments reduce one roadblock to metropolitan social solidarity, this does not mean that Swedes have a strong sense of attachment either to their metropolitan areas or to those areal units that in geographic scale lie between the metropolitan area and the local neighborhood. Save for seemingly strong attachments to and identification with "Mother Sweden" (which, after all, is in population about the size of an average American state), plus a strong attachment to "region of origin" (Småland, Värmland, and so on), it is accurate to say, in my opinion, that metropolitan Swedes are peculiarly detached from all territorially based units. Ties to place of employment can be quite strong, and the density of voluntary associations is easily the equivalent of that in the United States and Britain, but "community" does not have a strong local or areal connotation for metropolitan Swedes. They are more metropolitanwide and even suprametropolitan beings than are the urban dwellers of the other countries.

These characteristics of social structure in the Swedish metropolitan community are expressed politically through very low levels of local political participation. Swedes simply do not involve themselves in locally based politics to anywhere near the same degree as do the urban dwellers of the United States and Britain. This helps to preserve politics, for better or worse, for the experts and other members of the elite, but it also deprives

Swedes of a major source of community participation. In Sweden, political sensibilities are focused mainly at the national level, where, however, the chance for direct political participation by the person in the street is even less than at the local level.

The character of the metropolitan community in Sweden also may be associated with a sense of rootlessness. Local attachments are a primary source of personal identification and sense of belonging. And the metropolitan Swede is not infrequently portrayed as relatively detached and rootless, even lonely, as we shall see.

*The United States*

Metropolitan areas in the United States are unique among advanced societies in the degree to which they are dominated by economic and market forces. Decisions that favor the public interest, as distinct from the narrower interests of buyers and sellers in the marketplace, are relatively infrequent, and in this, as in so many other respects, U.S. metropolitan areas are especially dissimilar from those of Sweden. It is not that government has played no role in determining the structure of metropolitan areas. Government-sponsored parks, public housing, and open-space preservation, to take a few examples, often run counter to the dominant economic concerns, but for the most part, as in the case of government aid for freeways, suburbanization, and most urban renewal, the public sector, when it does act, takes measures that tend to foster and promote the already powerful interests in the marketplace.[20]

Part of the reason for this state of affairs is that local government in metropolitan areas tends to be highly fragmented. The New York area alone, for example, contains something like 1,400 governmental units. It is very difficult for so fragmented a public sector to act in ways counter to the dominant economic interests. Moreover, government at every level has neither the power nor the financial resources that exist in Sweden. Even in areas like the Sunbelt, where local government often is considerably less fragmented than in New York, the public sector is not able to take a more active hand in metropolitan planning and development.[21]

Unlike among Swedes, there is on the part of Americans widespread antipathy toward civil servants, government control, and more than minimum taxation. Instead of respecting the public sector, Americans tend to believe that market forces are inherently good, that these forces themselves for the most part express the public interest, and that they represent a highly regarded kind of personal freedom.[22] In urban development, this personal freedom is expressed, for example, through the belief that individual property owners should be able generally to use and dispose of their property as they see fit. The freedom is by no means unlimited, but it is certainly much greater than that found in any other advanced industrial society.

In terms of the broad dimensions of metropolitan community structure, this set of political and economic circumstances generates a high turnover of land uses with correspondingly high residential and commercial mobility; rapid neighborhood change; the polarization of neighborhoods and other urban districts by income and wealth, leading to the development of slums and inner-city decay; minimal public support for mass transportation; and relatively uncontrolled urban growth.[23] But the foregoing is little more than a litany of U.S. metropolitan ills.

Underlying the matrix of problems is the fact that the social bond that ties most residents to their metropolitan area is very frail. The attachments of residents are not to the area as a whole but to a very circumscribed portion of it in which people are situated with others of their own social class and circumstance. The localized attachments not only are the result of the widespread residential segregation of people but also stem from many metropolitan subcommunities' being distinct political and social realities—much more so, for example, than is the case in Sweden. Class and age homogenization are thus compounded by local government units that, while fragmented from a metropolitanwide viewpoint, are believed by the typical resident to be accessible. Due to these circumstances, metropolitan Americans demonstrate considerably more local political awareness and activity than do metropolitan Swedes.[24]

In addition, ties to voluntary associations and to religious groupings tend to reinforce the local community ties that already exist for political and social reasons. The spirit of localism extends all the way to neighboring, which is a more concerted activity in metropolitan United States than it is in Sweden or England. So what may appear to U.S. metropolitan planners as a patchwork quilt of social embeddedness in small communities without any overarching structure of higher purpose or even rationality does help to provide for residents some measure of local identity and attachment in an otherwise mass society.

If one examines the U.S. situation in terms of trends rather than international comparisons, the picture does not appear so bright, as will be detailed in the chapter to follow. Each year metropolitan local communities seem to become increasingly segregated, with no corresponding growth in coordination at the metropolitanwide level. Thus the metropolis as a whole becomes ever less than the sum of its parts, and the possibilities grow apace for intrametropolitan social conflict and breakdown. Within each segregated subcommunity, moreover, life turns ever inward as the community erodes through high residential turnover, diminished spending on the few public facilities and services that are provided, and the general privatization of life that has been greatly enhanced on the U.S. scene by television, by the growth of violent crime in many metropolitan neighborhoods, and by the widespread use of that most private of transportation vehicles, the automobile.

There is one other important dimension of local communities in metropolitan United States that is pointed up by cross-national comparison: the cultural bonds that link people together. Culture refers here to the meanings and values that people share. The traditional American small town had a largely intact culture, that is, one consisting of a body of integrated meanings and values—in such areas as sexual relations, education, religion, the family, and national loyalty—that were deeply held and widely shared. Such cultural integration has been largely lost in many metropolitan local communities today, especially in the newer metropolitan areas of the South and West and in the newer sections of older metropolitan areas. Other than in the older cities of the East, with their ethnic ghettos, local areas within the U.S. metropolis tend to be very diverse in religion and national origin, as well as in subcultures based on differences in chosen life-styles. They are homogeneous in social class and racial terms, but the homogeneity often goes no further.

It is not at all unusual for the households of a single street in metropolitan United States each to be linked to a different religion and national origin. The linkage may be to subcultures that are still intact, even richly so, but the local community culture as a whole typically has a character of ambiguity and superficial accommodation. There is often no clear agreement, for example, on cultural norms to guide such everyday matters as sexual conduct, property maintenance, and child rearing. Class homogeneity and "Americanism" may generate a modest cultural integration, but the meanings and values thus shared often are shallow, and the integration itself is fragile and easily upset. For persons without a strong subculture with which to identify, and a great many are in this circumstance, the culture of the American metropolitan local community can be filled with no small degree of ambiguity and anxiety.

*England*

In the structure of its metropolitan communities, as in so many other respects, England falls about midway on a continuum between Sweden and the United States. Social attachments to local communities in English metropolitan areas are quite strong. London, for example, is known worldwide as a city of strong local neighborhoods in a pattern common to the United States but not to Sweden.[25] Much political activity centers around named neighborhoods and districts, and these localities typically send indigenous political leaders to common councils. Local neighborhood life is further enhanced by a relatively high rate of home ownership (55 percent), and by strong efforts to preserve and protect historic neighborhood institutions and facilities. Moreover, class segregation in metropolitan England is closer to the American than the Swedish pattern, providing yet another basis for local community life.[26]

Yet in its larger economic and political dimensions, the structure of metropolitan communities in England is closer to that of metropolitan communities in Sweden.[27] Due to consolidation, local political boundaries in England more closely approximate metropolitan functional areas than is the case in the United States. And the metropolitan functional areas themselves have been sharply contained, thus establishing distinctly bounded metropolitan communities that have a semblance of unity and integration.[28] Moreover, the public sector in general in England has much more power than its American counterpart in guiding metropolitan growth and development.[29] This power is reflected in the relatively high prestige of the English civil servant who, while not enjoying the autonomy found in Sweden, certainly does not face the level of scorn associated with U.S. political life.

The sense of attachment to their metropolitan areas seems quite strong among the English. The attachment is accentuated by the continuingly vigorous use of the central cities for shopping and recreation (outlying, automobile-oriented shopping centers are comparatively rare in Britain), and by the maintenance of mass transportation at a high standard to the detriment of the private automobile, thus minimizing the automobile's centrifugal effects on social life.

The strong metropolitan attachment is complemented at the same time by a relatively rich local neighborhood life.[30] Community life in England is more pedestrian-oriented than in Sweden or the United States, forcing a high density of facilities and services in the immediate vicinity of people's houses. This generates an everyday life of intimacy and friendliness, especially in shopping activities, that is not found in the other countries. While neighboring appears not to be as important a social phenomenon as it is in the United States,[31] the English people being rather more reserved and private, pride in home and the proximate environment is every bit as strong, if not stronger, leading to high standards of residential maintenance. Neighborhood life in England, if not neighboring, is further enhanced by low residential turnover, so that the same neighborhood dwellers tend to be together over a great many years, generating a sense of solidarity. And having been the first nation to urbanize, many urban neighborhoods in England have very long traditions, indeed, on which feelings of solidarity may focus.

In many (but certainly not all) metropolitan neighborhoods in England one finds cultural integration at a level far above that in the United States. English culture is still very largely intact, with ethnic homogeneity remaining in many local areas. Despite the social-class mixing in local areas at a level above that of the United States, class lines are still relatively rigid and accepted, and social interaction is class bound along traditional lines, rather than being the search for common denominators that it often tends to be in the United States. Such class boundedness, of course, is a trait for which the English are often sharply criticized.

For all of these reasons, neighborhood life in the typical English metropolitan neighborhood contains less social conflict than is the case in the United States. Bickering over such things as norms of adult behavior, methods of child rearing, and the upkeep of property, for example, appears considerably diminished by U.S. standards. As was discussed in the last chapter, this contributes to a social comfort and contentedness in English life that is quite high, the low material level of living notwithstanding.

Metropolitan life in England, therefore, comes perhaps closest among the advanced societies to an ideal of rich local communities contained within a framework of metropolitan services in such a way that the two geographic levels complement rather than compete with each other. This may be the urban equivalent of having your cake and eating it too. Yet one fears that whatever success England has had in this regard comes partly, and perhaps largely, at the expense of material advancement. English life *is* materially primitive compared to the United States and Sweden. It is not out of line to argue that if a higher standard of living were in some way to be achieved, this delicate metropolitan balance would be upset, with a strong drift either in the U.S. or the Swedish directions. If we are really entering an era marked by the end of economic growth in advanced societies, such further material advancement might never come. But in that case, the division of economic spoils in a "zero-sum" society could create social conflict of other and unforeseen kinds.

Even without an economic trigger, significant metropolitan community change may come about in another way. England is increasingly, like the United States, a land of immigrants. In addition, the age and condition of English housing requires vast urban residential redevelopment, some of which has already taken place. Because so much of the English housing supply is publicly funded, new housing areas in redeveloped metropolitan centers tend toward relatively high levels of ethnic and social class mixing. Thus the neighborhood homogeneity of England is constantly being curtailed. While not without social benefits of another sort, this diminution of homogeneity, as much as economic change, could upset the current social balance in English metropolitan community life.

## Summary of Metropolitan Community Structure in Advanced Societies

In opening this chapter we described the characteristic structure of metropolitan communities in advanced societies, the structure that makes these areas historically unique among the world of communities. In the explanation of structural diversity among the three advanced nations, some variations on the main metropolitan themes were noted. The Swedish metropolis comes closest to being a "whole" community in its rational correspondence among functional, political, and social bonds. Yet this rationality may be secured at the cost of diminished social solidarity at the level of the neighborhood and other local environs. In a human-centered evaluation, one could reasonably hold that the macrogains in efficiency and rationality are not worth the local-level social costs. This view is backed by the impression of most observers that many metropolitan Swedes, despite the rationality of their macroenvironment, would like to leave the metropolitan area entirely for places regarded as being at a more human scale, places with a richer local community life. This desire seems little different in magnitude from that expressed in the United States.

The United States has managed to hold onto a larger measure of local community in the metropolis. Indeed, urban local-community sentiment has made up a very prominent part of U.S. political ideology, and there is little evidence of its lessening. But the local communities themselves are eroding. And one may reasonably conclude that on balance Americans pay a high price for this local community rectitude in the overall irrationality of U.S. metropolitan areas. A wise and all-powerful planner, starting afresh, would surely not design American metropolitan communities in their present form but, rather, would find some better matchup among economic, political, and social interconnections. The negative impact of the American metropolitan system on the lives of the middle class may not be so severe, but the system clearly exacerbates conditions at the underside of metropolitan life, where housing decay, crime and delinquency, family instability, and neighborhood conflict are all much more virulent than in the European counterparts.

At first glance England appears to have achieved a relatively workable and socially satisfactory balance among the competing structures of community life. Yet one must ask whether or not this is mainly due to Britian's lagging economic development, which is years behind the other two countries. Nonetheless, and despite their lower material level of living, the English have expressed through opinion polls a comparatively high satisfaction with their lives, including their overall community situation.[32] This may well be due, in part, to the structural characteristic of the English metropolitan setting.

Despite these significant variations among the metropolitan areas of the three nations, one underlying trend can be discerned that appears more than anything else to be shaping the character of metropolitan life wherever that life occurs. That trend is privatization; the magnification of the private in life and the diminution of the public. While the privatization of life is expresed somewhat differently in Sweden than it is in the United States, and it could be said to be less fully evolved in England than in the other two countries, the trend nonetheless seems to be the single most influential factor in distinguishing metropolitan life from its predecessors. It is to a close examination of this trend, and its consequences, that we now turn.

## Notes

1. A classic statement is M. Webber, "Order in Diversity: Community without Propinquity," in *Neighborhood, City and Metropolis*, ed. R. Gutman and D. Popenoe (New York: Random House, 1970).
2. See Allan Pred, *City-Systems in Advanced Economies* (London: Hutchinson, 1977); and L.S. Bourne, *Urban Systems* (London: Oxford University Press, 1975).
3. The conceptual scheme presented in this chapter draws on two main sources: Alvin Boskoff, *The Sociology of Urban Regions*, 2d ed. (New York: Meredith, 1970); and James Coleman, "Community Disorganization and Urban Problems" in *Contemporary Social Problems*, ed. R.K. Merton and R. Nisbet, 4th ed. (New York: Harcourt Brace Jovanovich, 1976), plus the works of T. Parsons and H.C. Bredemeier.
4. Boskoff, *Sociology of Urban Regions*, p. 143.
5. Ibid.
6. Ibid.
7. A classic statement of metropolitan political bargaining is N. Long, "The Local Community as an Ecology of Games," in Gutman and Popenoe, *Neighborhood, City and Metropolis*.
8. Coleman, "Community Disorganization and Urban Problems," pp. 559-68.
9. A classic statement of the deleterious effects of the decline of local communities is Robert A. Nisbet, *Community and Power* (New York: Oxford University Press, 1962). See also Bert E. Swanson, *The Concern for Community in Urban America* (New York: Odyssey Press, 1970).
10. Thomas J. Anton, *Governing Greater Stockholm* (Berkeley: University of California Press, 1975).
11. Ella Ödmann and Gun-Britt Dahlberg, *Urbanization in Sweden* (Stockholm: Allmänna Förlaget, 1970).
12. J. Board, *The Government and Politics of Sweden* (Boston: Houghton Mifflin, 1970).
13. Steven Kelman, *Regulating America, Regulation Sweden* (Cambridge: MIT Press, 1981); and T. Anton, *Administered Politics* (Boston: Martinus Nijhoff, 1980).
14. *Fact Sheet: Sweden: Local Government in 1976* (Stockholm: Swedish Information Service).

15. T. Anton, "Policy Making and Political Culture in Sweden," *Scandinavian Political Studies* 4 (1969).
16. Roland Huntford, *The New Totalitarians* (New York: Stein & Day, 1972).
17. Gerald D. Suttles, *The Social Construction of Communities* (Chicago: University of Chicago Press, 1972).
18. Richard F. Tomasson, *Sweden: Prototype of Modern Society* (New York: Random House, 1970), Ch.8.
19. Ibid., ch.3.
20. Two interesting accounts of the U.S. urban development are Richard F. Babcock, *The Zoning Game* (Madison: University of Wisconsin Press, 1969); and Constance Perin, *Everything in Its Place* (Princeton: Princeton United Press, 1977).
21. For an influential statement about metropolitan local government, see Scott Greer, *Governing the Metropolis* (New York: Wiley, 1962).
22. See Arnold J. Heidenheimer et al., *Comparative Public Policy* (New York: St. Martin's Press, 1975).
23. See Bruce Headey, *Housing Policy in the Developed Economy* (New York: St. Martin's Press, 1978).
24. See Heidenheimer et al., *Comparative Public Policy*, ch.9.
25. Steen Eiler Rassmussen, *London: The Unique City* (Cambridge: MIT Press, 1934).
26. For a good discussion of the urban sociology of London, see Michael Young and P. Willmott, *The Symmetrical Family* (New York: Penguin Books, 1973).
27. The variation in economic levels *among* English metropolitan areas is much greater than in Sweden, however, and more like the United States. See David Donnison with Paul Soto *The Good City* (London: Heinemann, 1980).
28. Peter Hall et al., *The Containment of Urban England* (London: Allen & Unwin, 1973).
29. An excellent discussion of U.S.-English differences is Marion Clawson and Peter Hall, *Planning and Urban Growth: An Anglo-American Comparison* (Baltimore: John Hopkins, University Press, 1973).
30. The classic studies of this are Michael Young and P. Willmott, *Family and Kinship in East London* (London: Routledge & Kegan Paul, 1957); and Peter Willmott and M. Young, *Family and Class in a London Suburb* (London: Routledge and Kegan Paul, 1960).
31. H.E. Bracey, *Neighbors: Subdivision Life in England and the United States* (Baton Rouge: Louisiana State University Press, 1964); and Graham A. Allen, *A Sociology of Friendship and Kinship* (Winchester, MA: Allen & Unwin, 1979).
32. In a 1981 international Gallup Poll, 84 percent of United Kingdom respondents stated that they were either "very satisfied" or "fairly satisfied" in answer to the question: "On the whole, how satisfied are you with the life you lead?" For comparison, the percentages in several other European nations were as follows (United States and Sweden were not included): Belgium, 85 percent; Denmark, 95 percent; Germany, 77 percent; France, 70 percent; Italy, 67 percent; Greece, 58 percent. Survey Research Consultants, *Index to International Public Opinion: 1980-81* (Westport, CT: Greenwood Press, 1982).

# PART IV
# CHANGE

# 7

# The Metropolitan Community and the Privatization of Life

"To live an entirely private life means above all to be deprived of things essential to a truly human life."[1] Hannah Arendt penned these words in the 1950s. She was bemoaning the loss in modern society of the public realm, the realm that "gathers us together and yet prevents our falling over each other."[2] In her work, and that of others who pursue the same theme, the metropolitan community is not singled out as a special locus; the privatization of life is regarded as a general feature of modern societies.[3] There is no denying that privatization is a product of centuries of social and cultural change, has multiple causes, and pervades almost every one of life's spheres. But I shall argue that privatization reaches its apogee in metropolitan communities *because of factors that are indigenous to those communities*. The many structural features of metropolitan communities reviewed in earlier chapters—their large and diverse populations, great geographic and functional differentiation of people and human activities, and weak local autonomy as political and social entities—make up a social and cultural climate in which there is a progressive diminution of public life and a magnification of private life to a degree that is both historically unprecedented and socially harmful.

*Privatization* is a rather ugly term, and one that unfortunately also has several meanings. The meaning I intend is straightforward: the growth of the private at the expense of the public, where the public is defined as "of, pertaining to, or affecting a population or a community as a whole." The private realm, or privatism, means "having nothing to do with public life," "not intended to be made publicly known," "away from public notice."[4] The essential nature of the metropolitan community, in my judgment, is one in which public activities and sentiments are curtailed and the community as a whole is organized mainly to foster private pursuits.

As suggested in the last few chapters, privatization is broadly found in each of the three metropolitan settings that have been the focus of this work, although with slightly different features and causes, depending upon each society's unique history and characteristics. Privatization is an extremely complex issue, and a full understanding of intersocietal differences must await further comparative research. Some of the differences, and the reasons for them, will be suggested later in this chapter. To begin, let us look at some ways in which privatization is expressed in modern life in general (with particular reference to the United States) through examining the changing character of three human activities that once pulled people out of their private spheres and into the public domain: work, shopping, and leisure.

## The Changing Character of Human Activities

### Work

Apart from their immediate households and close friends (and in the United States, for many, their churches) the strongest social tie for most citizens of modern societies is to their place of work. It is mainly through work that they are bound to society and make some contribution to the human population around them. Most people see life as two distinct social worlds—the world of work, and the private world of home and leisure. The two worlds are increasingly distinct in fact, and it is expected and desired that this be so. "I don't care anything about what you do in your private life as long as you perform your work satisfactorily" is the sentiment of a modern work manager that points up this issue. Work has left not only the home but the private world entirely.

Yet if work is still a public bond, it is surely a rather restricted and emphemeral one. It is abruptly severed at the end of each workday, as we retreat again into our private worlds, and it is continually subject to termination, especially as advanced societies enter a period of economic stagnation and perhaps decline. For many, a particular job has become one of the less stable elements in their lives. Even without a stagnant economy the durability of the work bond is always a suspect thing. In the capitalist economies of metropolitan societies, organizational loyalty to workers is continually discarded in the search for higher corporate profits, and worker loyalty to organizations is greatly compromised by the strong emphasis placed on individual advancement and therefore job mobility. These traits are of course more evident in the American than in the Swedish system.

Even with more stability and durability, however, the work bond in metropolitan societies would fail to meet any stern test of "publicness." In their attitudes toward work, the citizens of these societies do not emphasize work's public nature or contribution. Rather, they view work as a necessary means to a more rewarding personal, private life. People work because they have to—they need the money to be able to pursue the kind of private life they desire. Looked at in slightly different terms, metropolitan societies have shifted from an ethic of production to an ethic of consumption. We work not so much to produce, much less to improve the community, as to be able to consume. In turn, our personal identities are framed not so much by what we produce, as was the case with the small-town craftsman, as by what we consume: the houses and neighborhoods we are able to live in, the cars we drive, and the clothes we wear. Work is not an end in itself; it is a means to an end.

Now these ideas about the nature of modern work are in no sense new. They have been expressed by numerous social commentators since the beginning of the industrial revolution. But they remain an important insight about the modern world, and especially the world of the metropolitan area. There are many exceptions, most notably the professional classes whose lifetime "careers" and sometimes even job tenure signify a different perspective on work. But professionalization has not been carried far enough to reorder the lives of the great majority of metropolitan dwellers, and the professional classes themselves are by no means immune from the ethic of consumption.

*Leisure*

If work is no longer a very public endeavor, what about its opposite, leisure? Like work, leisure was at one time a far more public activity than it is today. Consider television, the leisure of first choice of most citizens in these societies. Television is one of the most solitary and privatized leisure-time activities that exists; it is a medium that totally absorbs one's senses, leaving little room for sociability even if viewed in the presence of others.

Much has been written about the direct psychological effects of television viewing, but often overlooked in studies of the impact of television are the forms of leisure that television has displaced.[5] Many of the displaced leisure forms are far more social and public than is television, such as neighboring, taking walks in the local community, and sitting on the porch and watching (and to some extent interacting with) the passing scene. These absent leisure forms explain, as well as anything else, why the typical metropolitan neighborhood scene in these societies today, especially in the suburbs, appears relatively lifeless, bereft of visible people, and turned inward upon itself.

Going to the movies and to mass spectator sports also express well the theme of privatized leisure, the one of a kind of escape from social reality into the darkness of a theater, the other a temporary suspension of social reality into the anonymity of the crowd. Neither involves any kind of sustained social relationship with a larger group or public, although each may take place in the presence of close, private companions. Privatized, too, has become the summer vacation, often a driving trip or charter flight with a small number of intimates (although the characteristic Swedish family gatherings at a summer home run counter to this trend).

Especially in the United States, with its relatively spacious detached homes with large yards, many leisure and recreational activities that once were communal in nature now take place within the privacy of the domicile. The widespread presence of the basement recreation or "rec" room together with the rear yard containing children's play equipment and perhaps even a small swimming pool ensure that many adults as well as children can recreate in their own private worlds, eschewing the necessity of venturing forth into a larger social orbit. In many American communities this privatization of recreation has led directly to the demise of leisure-oriented public facilities (which in turn sharply affects the lives of those who cannot afford the panoply of private facilities). In the newer U.S. Sunbelt cities particularly, where the privatization of recreation is much in evidence, the public provision of community recreational facilities is, by European standards, in very short supply.

To be sure, the privatization of recreation in the American middle class is not something regarded by the average citizen in a negative light. Few who can afford it turn their backs on this trend, for it gives an individual greater freedom of use and choice, and it provides parents with a greater measure of security regarding their children's safety. Yet at the same time this trend carries the insidious implication of cutting off people still further from community life and contact with others.

*Shopping*

The third human activity that traditionally has pulled people from their private worlds and into the public domain, is shopping. The marketplace was once a rich locus of social interaction and community contact and shopping was a highly communal activity. A residue of this tradition can still be found in British urban areas. In the other nations, however, shopping has become a highly impersonal and individualistic pursuit, with none of the comradeship and ritual with which it was once imbued. In American metropolitan areas shopping has become a once-a-week automobile trip to a distant place (such as a large shopping mall), where the activity seldom has any but a purely commercial purpose and is to be conducted with dispatch (the shopping behavior of some contemporary adolescents is an exception).

The changing nature of shopping was pointed up in a comparison in twelve California cities of 28 supermarkets and 12 farmers' markets. Of

900 supermarket shoppers, only 16 percent shopped with other adults; of the 248 farmers' markets' patrons, 75 percent did. Only one out of ten of the supermarket shoppers who were not with other adults chatted sociably with other customers, compared to two out of three of the farmers' market shoppers.[6]

How is privatization accentuated by the metropolitan community? The form and social structure of the metropolitan community contribute to the privatization of life through two main characteristics: demographic makeup and differentiation of activities. The first of these was emphasized in the classic work of the sociologist Louis Wirth.[7] Demographically, the metropolitan community is defined by the key variables of scale and diversity. A large number of people are living in a limited area, and the people tend to be quite diverse, having been drawn from a wide range of local community cultures and sometimes different ethnic and racial groups. Because of these key demographic facts, there develops in metropolitan areas a feeling of public estrangement among residents that is not found in smaller and more homogeneous places. Not only are most of the people with whom the metropolitan dweller comes into daily contact in public life total strangers but many are often markedly different in appearance and behavior as well.[8]

Public estrangement naturally makes it more difficult for people to relate in public. To cope with anonymity and diversity, people necessarily become more wary of others, less open; they "stick to their own business" in a way that may be seen as unfriendliness. In short, they withdraw more into their own private, known worlds where they feel more secure and at home.[9]

Of course most people are able to adapt to a life among strangers. The coping mechanisms they develop, such as limiting the emotional contact they have with others in public, enable them to function quite well and with a minimum of stress. But the coping mechanisms serve to further differentiate the public and private worlds.[10] Metropolitan dwellers come to make an especially sharp distinction between the limited private world of their family, friends, and acquaintances, and the public world of strangers. A different set of manners and customs becomes established for each world, one based on intimacy and feeling and the other on impersonal exchanges and formal codes of conduct.

As metropolitan areas grow in scale and diversity, the private worlds necessarily take on even more significance for people. In the United States particularly, high rates of metropolitan crime further encourage a private withdrawal.[11] The public world becomes one not only of anonymity and diversity but of disorder, a world wherein a climate of fear of personal injury develops. In its extreme form such a public world can become one where public order is at a premium, the world consisting essentially of little more than a set of private realms loosely strung together. The inner-city areas of some American metropolitan regions might be said to closely approach, from time to time, this extreme social form.

The second characteristic of the metropolitan community that helps to break down the public realm is the great geographic and functional differentiation of human activities. In plain terms, this means that human activities—such as domestic living, work, shopping, and leisure—take place in organizations and spaces that are specialized for that purpose and physically located some distance apart from each other. In the traditional village activities took place virtually on top of one another, and there was a profound overlap among them. In the metropolis, the opposite is the case.

A high degree of differentiation has always been a characteristic of urban as distinct from rural places. Writing about Philadelphia, a town of 23,700 on the eve of the Revolution, Sam B. Warner in *The Private City* emphasizes the tremendous diversity of occupations, social classes, and ethnic groups.[12] But the differentiation had not yet led to separation, and the overlap among activities had very positive implications. "The real secret of the peace and order of the eighteenth-century town lay not its government but in the informal structure of its community," notes Warner. "The community had been created out of a remarkably inclusive network of business and economic relationships and it was maintained by the daily interactions of trade and sociability".[13] "It was the unity of everyday life, from tavern, to street, to workplace, to housing, which held the town and its leaders together in the eighteenth century. This unity made it possible for the minority of Revolutionary merchants, artisans, and shopkeepers to hold together, run the town, and manage a share of the war against England, even in the face of Quaker neutrality and Tory opposition."[14]

Such "unity of everyday life" is remarkably absent in the metropolis. In what Peter Berger has called "the pluralization of life worlds," the social worlds of home, work, shopping, and leisure are not only pursued for private ends but conducted in isolation from one another.[15] Far from providing the metropolitan community with any kind of unity, they lead to public breakdown and the further encapsulation of metropolitan dwellers in mostly private worlds.

The "pluralization of life worlds" shows up very clearly in studies of the social networks in metropolitan life. One way of classifying peoples' social networks—the set of people with whom an individual regularly is involved—is in terms of structural attributes ranging from close-knit to loose-knit.[16] A close-knit (or dense) network is one in which the various people in an individual's network also know and interact with each other. A principal finding of metropolitan network analysis is that metropolitan citizens tend to have very loose-knit (low-density) relationships. That is, their relationships are spread among several different worlds—work, leisure, church, family—and the people in these separate worlds typically do not even know, much less interact with, one another.[17] Thus not only have the main activities of everyday life become privatized but so have the circles of friends and acquaintances.

### The Privatization of Space in Metropolitan Communities

If our activities and social contacts have become privatized, one can readily assume that the spaces in which these activities take place have also garnered a more private character—that much community space over time has shifted from public to private. This, in fact, is precisely what has happened. Contrast, for example, the deeply private feel of a wealthy American suburb, where households live behind the protection of fence, hedge, or wall, venturing forth only within the confines of a motorized enclosed box, with the bustling street life of a medieval city or the communal interaction of a small town "green," where private household and public space appear effortlessly to spill over into one another.

It is in the privatization of space, because it is so tangible and visible, that the breakdown of the public realm in metropolitan life can most clearly be seen. The American suburb is the extreme case, but privatization is a dominant motif in most of the other ecological zones of the metropolis as well. Streets and sidewalks that once provided public pedestrian interaction and even entertainment have for the most part been abandoned to the utter privacy of the automobile; public parks have fallen into disuse and misuse; town squares have become the mostly ornamental appendages of commercialism. The American metropolitan apartment dweller lives behind locked doors, using public space mainly as a means of access and egress to desired private loci, not as space in which to linger and utilize for its own sake (save, perhaps, for during the lunch hour at work). And where is the public space in a Houston or a Los Angeles? It does exist, but is overwhelmed by the dominance of essentially private spheres.

Public space in Europe is of course not only more abundant but also more utilized. This points up the exaggerated privatization of American communities. But the long-run trend in Europe seems similar to that found in the United States—public action has prevented the American extreme, yet over time more and more of the spatial backdrop to metropolitan life is losing its public character.

The privatization of space can be traced well back into Western history, and the reasons for it are many and varied.[18] Certainly the trend is associated with the long-run movement toward individualism, in which the individual's desire for autonomy is reflected in a desire for space that can be claimed as one's own, space in which one can do as one wishes without the intrusion of others. Even within the home it is not hard to discern the trend toward private rooms and lockable doors, providing residents with that extreme form of privacy called isolation.

The privatization of space is also promoted by affluence. It takes money to be able to afford to have private space, and in affluent, advanced industrial societies private space is clearly more affordable for a large number of people. And like so many other material things that are available through purchase, having more of them brings one higher personal status. Indeed, the amount of private space one owns is a significant measure of status in each of these societies, whether it be the size of one's office at work or the size of one's house or apartment.

One of the inescapable facts behind the relative intractability of the trend toward the privatization of space is each person's basic desire for more space rather than less. Other things equal, it is the rare person who will turn down a larger room for a smaller one, a more spacious dwelling unit for a less spacious one, or a private yard for no yard at all. Of course strong public and economic limits can be placed on such choices, and space is a finite quantity. But where space is relatively abundant, and public and economic limits are weak, as in the United States, community spatial patterns are very much the product, for the most part unintended, of millions of such private spatial choices.

In metropolitan communities the privatization of space stems from much more than such individual preferences, however. We spoke above about the subjective feelings of withdrawal that result from the public estrangement in metropolitan life. This withdrawal is not only subjective but profoundly spatial in its manifestations.

It is difficult for community life to function in the face of high anonymity—the situation where many of the people met in daily life are unknown to us. Urban dwellers somehow must find ways partially to personalize the anonymous urban scene, to make at least tentative identifications of strangers in the urban public space and thus cause the urban world to be to some extent predictable. In traditional preindustrial urban settings, as noted by Lyn Lofland in *A World of Strangers*, the use of public space was by modern standards almost chaotic, but the chaos was tempered by what she calls appearential ordering.[19] In contacts with strangers, one could develop some sense of who they were by how they looked—especially what clothes they wore. Members of the various social classes were identifiable, so were members of guilds, ranks of the church hierarchy, and so on. And just as important as these appearential codes was the fact that the relationship among the different types of people was very closely regulated by social norms. There were clearly prescribed ways of acting toward people based on the appearential signals that they gave off. In the modern city, by contrast, "appearances are chaotic, space is ordered."[20] There has been not only a deterioration of symbols of status but also a weakening of the norms governing the relationships among different categories of people. There are more strangers than ever, but we find it much more difficult to know how to act toward them. One solution to this dilemma has been to spatially order people as never before.

We have already discussed at length the tremendous spatial ordering of the modern metropolis, the high degree to which people and activities of certain types are in specialized districts. From a personal point of view, an underlying rationale for this spatial ordering is that it is one way to resolve the problem of the stranger: where appearances are deceptive and norms are weak, distance can be put between self and stranger. If people of different types are housed in distinct areas, geographically apart from one another, the chances of contact among them are minimized.

Thus, metropolitan dwellers retreat into semiprivate spheres that are geographically separate from the private worlds of others who are unlike themselves. The metropolis becomes a vast mosaic of small, relatively semiprivate spatial worlds, whether they be the rich person's suburban refuge, the poor person's urban ghetto, the ethnic's "urban village," or the vast tracts of comfortable lower-middle-class housing that fall in between.

As the suburbanites, the underclass, the ethnic villagers, and the middle masses become more and more encapsulated in their semiprivate spheres, the public spaces that might bind them together, the common meeting grounds, tend to atrophy. Central Park in New York City, a place of fear that is virtually closed at night, is perhaps the best-known example of this tendency. It is not only that Central Park is perceived as crime ridden but also that its very publicness causes apprehension. Because it cannot be contained within any single semiprivate sphere, and thus is truly accessible to all members of the public, the issue of coping with anonymity in Central Park becomes immense, and more than many wish to face.

How different it is in the public spaces, such as parks and playgrounds, that are located in the homogeneous, semiprivate zones of the metropolis. A suburban park or playground may be "public," for example, but it is surely not regarded as a proper place for the leisure pursuits of unlike persons from distant metropolitan places. Even if such places are state owned, and thus legally accessible to all, local residents typically attempt to maintain them in a semiprivate condition through a variety of informal social pressures. Outsiders are made to feel unwelcome. The same holds true for public streets used as pedestrian zones, and for many public places of amusement. Public in name only, such places typically become the semiprivate locale of the locals, whose underlying reason is to achieve some minimum sense of security and "at-homeness" in an otherwise anonymous world.

In theory, the "downtown" area is the common public meeting ground for metropolitan residents. But as is well known, in the United States it has atrophied more than any other metropolitan segment, and become in numerous cities but a pale shadow of its former being. With the outflow of people, jobs, and shopping, many central cities (of course there are notable exceptions) have become merely daytime centers for people going about their daily business. At night they virtually shut down, the leisure and other nonwork activities having long since retreated to the mosaic of semiprivate and private worlds on the periphery.

The broad trend we have been discussing, the spatial ordering of the metropolis into semiprivate segments, might be thought to enhance the public character of peoples' lives within each segment, albeit at the expense of the metropolis as a whole. This is indeed the implication of the underlying rationale discussed above, and there can be no doubt that this trend has made the metropolis a more livable environment for millions of people. Yet if the trend applies in the metropolitanwide sphere, it also appears to apply in the smaller segments. If these segments grow in anonymity, people will retreat still further into ever more private worlds. This is exactly what has been happening.

For two reasons many homogeneous segments of the metropolis are becoming more anonymous places with each passing year. First, the high rate of residential mobility (especially in the United States) has ensured a constant turnover of the population. As attempts to integrate new people into the community erode from this high turnover, near neighbors become "strangers next door." Second, homogeneity gives way to heterogeneity as the high residential turnover involves not just a replacement of residents but the introduction into the community of different types of people. The working class moves into middle-class areas, singles into family areas, Catholics into Protestant areas, and blacks into white areas. Each of these moves is eminently justifiable on many moral as well as legal grounds, but nonetheless its effect is to increase the anonymity and public apprehension within each area, and thus force people to withdraw further into their homes and yards, their churches, their private clubs, and their loose-knit social networks.

One other element of the American metropolitan scene—the automobile—must be reemphasized because it so effectively permits the disparate private worlds to function while at the same time causing atrophy in the public sphere. In total privacy, the automobile user shuttles back and forth among private places, never in fact having to "go public." An automobile intrusion into semiprivate space, such as a local neighborhood street, is very different from a pedestrian intrusion. For the automobile user, one's private space is never really left. And in the automobile-oriented world, public interaction in space almost ceases to exist.

### The Decline in Expression of Public Solidarity

In view of all these powerful forces of privatization, one additional indicator of the breakdown of the public realms in metropolitan communities should come as no surprise. There appears to be a progressive decline in public expressions of community solidarity and togetherness in the form of public parades, town festivals, and other public celebrations. Part of the reason is that many metropolitan municipalities simply are not physically arranged properly for such events—they have no main street, for example; others are too new, too small, or too heterogeneous to constitute viable communities of the kind that lend themselves to public expression. Whatever the reasons, and they are numerous, the modern metropolitan dweller has little firsthand experience with the public parades and festivals that once provided a sense of cohesion to most groupings of people living in the same geographic locality.

Attendance at metropolitan sports events provides some diversion from private worlds, but the character and meanings expressed at the events are not very similar to a small-town parade. And some metropolitan areas have a Mardi Gras, or its equivalent, but the scale and commercialization of such an event often removes it quite far from the celebration of solidarity. There remain few equivalents at the local level of what we see nationally over television, such as the inauguration of the president, or the funeral of a famous public figure. In some ways, perhaps, television has brought us together nationally, but the expression of solidarity among the people who live near us is an ever-fleeting reality.

### The Virtues of Privatization

If the privatization of life is conceived as the insulation of the individual from many of the pressures of the crowd, the protection from the tyrannies of public demand, then it must surely be regarded as one of the landmark achievements of Western civilization. By permitting individuals to achieve some distance from the groups into which they are born or otherwise involuntarily find themselves, privatization has fostered the development and dignity of the individual and in many ways has promoted the sum total of human happiness. But one can still ask, might not this trend, as observed in the metropolitan areas of advanced societies, have gone too far? Is it not possible that the unlocking of society and culture, in a way that fosters the pursuit of individual development and private pleasure, has reached a point where it has generated what could be called a public plight? I will argue that it has. But let us first be clear about the real virtues of privatization and the basic human need for privacy.

I will not dwell at length on the virtues of a privatized life. It is what the rich people of the world have always sought and usually had, at least for the past few centuries, and which modern society finally brought to the masses (still today, the higher the income and prestige levels, the greater the privatism in one's life). The persons are rare, at least in Western society, who would rather dwell in public space than in their own personal, private space; share a room with others than have a room of their own; share washing facilities with others than have their own washing machine; have their daily agenda be dictated by others than by themselves; be swallowed up by the group than be insulated from group pressures. Indeed, the value of privatism seems to grow with each passing year. For the generations that have been at least vicarious witness to the Nazi movement and the holocaust, the Stalinist tyrannies, the Chinese cultural revolution, and the genocide of Pol Pot, a private life, lived apart from the observations and dictates of the public, seems almost as necessary as eating and breathing.

Even aside from the issue of these dramatic group tyrannies, from people's right to be protected from the group, the case for privatism is a most compelling one. It can be summed up in three points:

1. By becoming free from some of the social pressures of others, individuals are able to be more creative, to show more initiative, to develop more fully their own native potentials. It is from such freedom that societies achieve cultural advance, whether in the arts, the sciences, or in moral and political development. This is the widely discussed freedom of city life, the reason that the growth of cities and the emergence of civilized life and civilization itself have long been regarded as virtually synonymous. Most great human advances have come from cities, where the social matrix, built on at least limited privatism, is one that stimulates innovation and change rather than suppressing it.

2. Innovation and creativity stem not only from people's being more on their own, and thus having to rely on self-initiative, but also from their being able to mix with diverse others of their own choosing. It is out of such mixtures that the critical masses of human energy develop that have led to many of the world's great social and cultural movements.

The ability to mix socially with persons of one's own choosing, freed from the involuntary ties of family and location into which an individual is born, can have profound personal as well as social benefits. For the individual born of low status who wishes to rise, born into a troubled family who wishes to escape, or born in a backwater area who wishes to migrate, a privatized society permits a fresh start in life and thus immeasurably advances the cause of human freedom. And even for the socially privileged, their free choice of friends and associates certainly brings them a large measure of human happiness compared to what their lives would be like without such freedom.

3. Finally, it is an inescapable reality that modern social settings, notably metropolitan areas, are made up of many different minority subcultures. There can be no doubt that such subcultures, if they are to thrive and even survive, require a social setting that is largely privatized, one where majority values cannot get a stranglehold on public and private life. Indeed, minority groups in the United States tend to gravitate to those urban centers, such as San Francisco, Los Angeles, and New York City, where privatization has been carried to the greatest extremes, where "live and let live" seems almost to be written into municipal codes. Both for their own development, and for the many contributions that minority groups make to American life, this advantage of privatization cannot easily be dismissed.

To take a stand against the overprivatization of metropolitan life, then, is in no sense to deny the great virtues of a relatively private life style, much less the great advances of Western civilization. It is, rather, to suggest that excessive privatization has many unintended consequences, consequences that are far from the minds of people as they quietly pursue their own private lives but that nonetheless are real and very important when viewed within the context of the larger community or public. The unintended consequences of privatization can be examined from two perspectives: that of the functioning and well-being of the community as a whole, and that of the personal well-being of each individual community member. Because the community perspective highlights the more obvious consequences, it is to that perspective we now turn.

### Privatization and the Functioning of Communities

First and foremost, excessive privatization seriously impedes the ability of a community to take collective action on common problems. The members of privatized communities come to focus their attention mainly on themselves and their immediate group of like-minded associates. The collective impulse, the feeling that the problems of people living nearby are to some extent also their problems, becomes attenuated. To take some familiar examples, in a system where most people rely exclusively on private automobiles as their means of personal transportation, the need for public, mass transportation on the part of those who cannot afford a car, or who cannot drive—children and young teenagers, the elderly, the sick and the disabled, and many poor people—is only dimly perceived. Or in a system that provides private backyards, recreation rooms, and even swimming pools for many people, the need for public leisure-time facilities and spaces for the large number of people who cannot afford such private advantages is largely pushed from the public mind. Or in settings where there are few families with young children, but where those children must be well educated if the community as a whole is to thrive, the costs of such education are often borne very grudgingly because of the inability to perceive a direct and immediate personal benefit.

Each of these examples is commonplace in American life, and however much this nation may be the land of private opportunity, it is also generally recognized as a society in which, at least relative to European counterparts, such public needs often fail to be met. It is not that American communities lack the resources to meet these needs but that an exaggerated sense of privatism leads the majority to feel either that public needs do not exist or that they somehow will (and should) be met privately.

The dearth of collective spirit can be a relatively benign consequence of privatism. As public needs become acute, somehow communities manage to muddle through, especially with the help of resources from state and federal governments (but these resources may dampen still further the local collective spirit!). A worse consequence is when the collective spirit becomes so weak that intergroup conflict arises—each group not only looks out primarily for its own but actively seeks to block the actions of other groups. Violent intergroup conflict has not become a common pattern in the American metropolis but it has occurred from time to time—notably in the late 1960s. In a less violent form, however, intergroup conflict—among races, classes, and subcultures—is the stuff of American urban and suburban life. Good examples are racial conflicts over housing, and class conflicts over welfare expenditures.

These political effects of privatization have long been the basic grist of American political criticism. They have been so thoroughly discussed, and over so many years, that it would be very difficult at this juncture to add much to the debate. Less widely discussed, however, have been the effects of privatism on what might be called the quality of public life. Especially in the United States, but also a tendency in the European countries, everyday public life in metropolitan communities has taken on a strong aura of fear and apprehension that goes well beyond the effects of urban anonymity. People are ever more fearful in their encounters with strangers in public places, ever more apprehensive about going outside the bounds of their private and semiprivate worlds and into the public sphere. The reason for this is the high rate of metropolitan street crime. In terms of people's personal perceptions, at least, metropolitan public life is no longer very safe, and this lack of safety frequently is felt even in that heart of private existence, the home. The causes of crime are terribly complex and still not very well understood. In multivariate analyses all kinds of factors related to crime have been isolated, ranging from poverty and economic deprivation through broken homes and bad parents to personal traits, both biological and social.[21] But a common "cause" turned up in many studies of crime and delinquency is the lack of social control. The term *social control* refers to social processes that condition or limit the actions of people to motivate them to conform to social norms. Such social processes range from the dirty look one person gives another to a life sentence at Sing Sing. Both processes are a way of saying, "Don't."[22]

In very small-scale, traditional societies, deviance of any kind is rare and conformity is at a maximum because the people agree on the group's norms, and these norms constantly are reinforced by all community members in the informal round of daily life. Social control becomes a much more serious problem in urban settings where, because of the presence of many strangers, newcomers, and people of diverse backgrounds, formal mechanisms must be set up to inform people of the norms (schools, churches) and to enforce them when necessary (police, courts, the correctional system). In such settings, the use of informal mechanisms of social control—the dirty look, the harsh words, the reporting of a person's actions to close associates—begin to decline in public places and become relegated only to people's private and intimate worlds, where all the members are known to one another. In the public sphere, social control is generally left up to agencies especially set up for that purpose. Compared to the eyes and ears of the community at large, however, these agencies are inherently inefficient; with limited numbers and short of a police state, they can deal only with the most serious forms of deviance, and even then must rely heavily on citizen support.

The inefficiency of formal social control agencies and processes could be said to promote the privatization of space and metropolitan areas. In their attempts to develop bounded neighborhoods where friends and strangers can be distinguished from one another—whether it be the ethnic urban village or the semiprivate suburb—metropolitan dwellers have come up with a partial solution to the problem. But such privatization is a partial solution at best, and in the long run no solution at all from the perspective of the community as a whole. Having an armed guard to limit access to an inner-city apartment building or to the walled subcommunities of the rich that are now found across the United States, to take some exteme examples, undoubtedly reduces the crime rate within those compounds, but it makes things worse for the rest of us for two reasons. First, it merely pushes criminal activity into the not-so-well-protected areas, perhaps the very areas where we ourselves are living, and second, it leads to the further attrition of *informal* social control mechanisms in public life. People who live that way have opted out of public life just as much as if they had left the community entirely; they no longer realistically care about what happens to anyone else.

Low crime rates in public settings are strongly related to people's willingness to *intervene* informally, even when total strangers are involved. People in public space must be willing to take action on their own to help out others in need, to report suspicious activities, to speak up to youth who have gotten out of line, and always to keep their eyes open. When many residents seldom even set foot in public space, as is the case with an automobile-oriented population, such intervention is virtually impossible. And even in many American pedestrian settings, public interaction has deteriorated so much that bystander intervention has become almost a thing of the past. Many times, people are unwilling even to anonymously call the police. And as they retreat more into their own private spaces, the situation worsens to the point where "It's a jungle out there" becomes more than a flip saying.[23]

Of course a high crime rate cannot be remedied through bystander intervention, nor could the lack of such intervention be said to be a main cause of crime. What I am trying to suggest is that those urban places that have a low crime rate—and there are many—tend to have a relatively rich public life in which people interact with and have concern for one another in public places. One thinks, for example, of London and Tokyo among the very large cities; at a smaller scale are a myriad of cities and towns spread all over the world.

The privatization of life is no doubt partially a response to a high crime rate, as can be seen clearly in the United States, but what needs to be emphasized is that at the same time it is a contributing factor to crime. By destroying public life, it destroys those threads of informal social control that are so necessary if a community as a whole is to persevere. Privatization can even be carried so far, to·be discussed below, that it destroys the fabric of people's private worlds, thus leaving them with little social control of any kind save for the societal threats of formal punishment if caught.

In summary, I suggest that excessive privatization has three very adverse consequences for the functioning of local communities: it seriously hampers the allocation of resources to meeting public needs; it generates group tensions that can lead to substantial intergroup conflict; and it promotes the growth of crime and delinquency. Now let us turn to the consequences for individual community members, the personal effects of living in an overly privatized world.

## The Changing Private World of Social Relationships

To this point we have been arguing that people in metropolitan areas have moved increasingly into their own private worlds, at no small cost to the quality of community life as a whole. And as the public world becomes more alien, metropolitan dwellers back off still further into their mostly self-created bastions of intimacy. We have so far been rather silent about the quality of life in these private bastions of intimate relationships, however. Are they providing people an adequate replacement for a more public life? Or is it the case, as Hannah Arendt wrote, that "it seems to be in the nature of the relationship between the public and private realms that the final state of the disappearance of the public realm should be accompanied by the threatened liquidation of the private realm as well."[24] Along similar lines, Christopher Lasch has stated: "When personal relations are conducted with no other object than psychic survival, 'privatism' no longer provides a haven from a heartless world. On the contrary, private life takes on the very qualities of the anarchic social order from which it is supposed to provide a refuge. It is the devastation of personal life, not the retreat into privatism, that needs to be criticised and condemned."[25] To begin, let us review the ways in which private social relationships are changing under the impact of metropolitan conditions, starting with the household.

### *The Household*

A household can be defined as one or more people who maintain a separate living unit (a unit having its own entrance or cooking facilities).[26] In 1790, about 6 people on the average maintained a separate living unit in the United States. After 140 years, in 1930, the average household size had dropped by one-third to 4 persons. But in only 50 years after that, the household size had dropped by another one-third to its current figure of about 2.7 persons. U.S. Census Bureau projections suggest a household size of just 2.3 persons by 1995.[27] The average household size in Britain is currently about the same as in the United States (2.8 in 1978), and in Sweden it is somewhat lower (2.3 in 1980).[28] These are national averages. In urban areas the household size is slightly lower; in Swedish urban areas, for example, the average household may now consist of fewer than two persons.

Another way of looking at household size is the percentage of households in which people live alone, now 22 percent of all households in the United

States and Britain, and 26 percent in Sweden. These figures do not include persons living in institutions, such as prisons, college dormitories, and nursing homes. Finding the current annual growth rate of single-person households an "astounding" 3.6 percent per year, a group of U.S. researchers refers to this trend as "one of the most profound but relatively neglected changes of recent decades."[29]

Many reasons are put forth to account for the sharp decline in household size, no one of which is predominant. The declining birthrate in these nations leads to smaller family sizes because the average woman has fewer children; the increasing number of the elderly in these populations, with the percentage over age 65 standing at 11 in the United States, 15 in the United Kingdom, and 16 in Sweden, generates many single-person households, especially of widows;[30] and the high divorce rates suggest an uncoupling of people into separate, smaller domiciles. To these reasons one must add the rising age at first marriage, associated with people's delaying the start of families and living separately or in pairs sometimes through their twenties. Also, the general affluence in these societies is a factor; it means that family members who in an earlier period would have been forced economically to share a household are now able to go out on their own. Indeed, the latter cause was given special emphasis by the research team noted above, which views "the decision to live alone as a reflection of an economic demand for privacy or autonomy," a demand that is increasingly capable of being met in advanced societies due to rising personal incomes.[31]

Whatever the reasons for the decline in size, a notable social dimension of the modern household is that the giving and sharing of daily domestic life, once involving a sizable number of people, now take place in a very tiny group. In a substantial and growing number of households, more than a quarter of all households in Sweden, there is in fact *no* other person in the same domicile with whom regularly to give, to share, and to communicate. It is certainly the case that some relationships formerly found within households have been transferred to persons outside the household, an issue to be explored below. But it cannot be denied that there is a very significant difference between living one's day-to-day domestic life—household management, meal preparation, leisure-time pursuits, intimate companionship—in a group of five, six, or seven people compared to just one or two others, or to no one at all. While the personal freedom that comes from being partially insulated from the dictates of others is one implication of smaller household size, at the same time the daily human needs for love relationships and other forms of human contact must often be met by a very limited number of people, a situation that can make such relationships especially intense and fragile.

It is not sheer numbers alone that are involved in the changing household but also a loss of social diversity. The 1790 U.S. household of six people was of a different character than the contemporary urban household in much more than size. It was typically a three-generation household with a very large age spread ranging from infancy to old age.[32] Further contact with people of a wide diversity of life stages and life-styles was provided by the entry and exit into the domicile for temporary periods of boarders, lodgers, servants, relatives, and friends. This provided a daily connection with many generations and a full round of life, a connection that today is more the stuff of movies and soap operas than of the average middle-class home.

*The Family and Kin Group*

Closely associated with the smaller and more homogeneous household is the decrease in size and the change in character of the typical family unit. Much has been written about the demise of the extended family, the type of family in which the husband-wife-children unit is extended with the addition of relatives, often of a different generation. Although the scope of the extended family system in Western civilization has been widely exaggerated,[33] it is nonetheless true that there has been an exceedingly steep drop in the percentage of three-or-more-generation families living under one roof, which today make up only about 5 percent of households.[34] As the generations have parted from a single domicile, so also have they increasingly become geographically separated, especially in the United States, leading to a decline in face-to-face contact among them.[35] The negative consequences often cited in the demise of the extended family include the "isolation" of the nuclear family and of the elderly, the generation gap, and the decline in household services, especially child care, formerly provided by the elderly.[36]

Few seem to regret the loss of the extended family, however. And even those who do are seldom found inviting their elderly parents to come back to live with them. In Britain and Scandinavia housing policies favor the location of grandparents in proximity to their children, at least in the same community, but there is scant interest in resurrecting the three-generation household. In the United States, such housing policies as exist tend to favor the permanent geographic separation of the generations; this is one of the few countries in the world where one finds a proliferation of separate communities for senior citizens, often located to provide geographic isolation and with no children allowed as permanent residents. Extremely common in the United States as well are the unplanned, age-segregated neighborhoods for the elderly in metropolitan areas, the result of market forces.

Sometimes lost in the discussion about extended families is another most significant and overlooked trend: the total size of each person's kinship group has greatly diminished in advanced societies. A kinship or kin group is "the group of people who do not all reside in a single household but are related by common ancestry or origin, or by marriage and adoption, and who recognize certain obligations and responsibilities toward one another." In brief, such groups are much smaller than they used to be, just as families and households are. As the size of each family drops, so does the total number of aunts, uncles, and cousins as well as brothers and sisters that each person has.

The main significance of this is suggested by the last clause in the formal definition of kinship given above: there are fewer persons for whom one has those *special familial obligations and responsibilities*. Because it yields no small measure of personal freedom from the demands of others whom one did not freely and voluntarily choose, many would regard this as a marked advantage. In this light family relationships are seen as a kind of social trap into which one is involuntarily born and from which extrication is most difficult. Yet of at least equal significance of the smaller kinship group for the individual is that *there are fewer persons from whom one can expect a special sense of obligation and responsibility*. The loss of obligations to others goes hand in hand with the loss of obligations that others have for you.

The key dimension of this issue is the essential distinction in character between kin and nonkin relationships.[37] Often these two types of relationships are treated by social scientists as simple alternatives for one another. But for the overwhelming majority of people throughout history, and I think still today, the two relationships are quite different in kind. Whether partly for innate biological reasons, as suggested by contemporary sociobiologists, or mostly due to cultural dictates, people *do* tend to feel a special sense of obligation and responsibility toward their close relatives that they do not feel toward mere friends. One can think of approaching many close relatives for a loan of money, for example, but this is a much less likely thought in regard to even the best of friends. This special economic linkage frequently shows up in the marketplace, where relatives help each other out, and in government, where the special tie between relatives has led to the strong enforcement of rules preventing nepotism. In the social sphere, children seem to have an affinity for relatives that is different for nonrelatives; relationships are established among cousins, for example, where heterogeneity would militate against such relationships if "blood ties" were not involved.

Because one is born to them, relationships among relatives are accepted by people as givens; they have naturalness and immutability that mark them as a special category. Relationships among nonrelatives, on the other hand, must be slowly developed and continually nurtured.[38] It takes a real effort to maintain them, and their tenure is notoriously subject to loss by geographic distance and by change in circumstance, a fact quickly attested to by an examination of an individual's Christmas card lists over the years, where friends can be seen to come and go in droves while relatives, no matter how distant, forever remain.

The decline in family and kin-group size in modern and especially urban settings, then, points up a noteworthy change in the character of social relationships. The urbanite may have as many social relationships as ever, indeed this is the conclusion of most empirical investigations,[39] but they become more difficult to maintain and thus are less durable. Adequate friendships can of course be preserved by socially skilled and persistent people. For the less socially graced, however, the urban competition for adequate friendships can be a debilitating experience, and one in which the losers have few relatives to fall back on in time of need. While the "loss of family" may be liberating for the socially strong, therefore, providing the opportunity for voluntary rather than mostly involuntary relationships with others, the loss can be seriously problematic for the socially weak, with the definite possibility of having no intimate relationships at all. For the person who at the same time lives alone, metropolitan life can become a very lonely and bleak endeavor.[40]

What about the quality of the family life that remains? So much has been written about the disarray in which the modern urban family finds itself that a summary here will perhaps only restate the obvious. The overwhelming majority of the populations in these three societies do marry and form a family sometime in their lives, and most of the people at any one time are living in an intact and one supposes reasonably contented family unit. Nevertheless, the structure of the family continues to undergo substantial modification as the divorce rates increase, the percentage of single-parent families approaches 20 percent of all families in the United States, and the turnover of intimate partners that a single person has during a lifetime goes up. It may be that this switching of family partners has led many adults into happier personal lives, and that what are often the mistakes of youth are no longer irrevocable and uncorrectable. Yet one can find few children who take such a benign view of the high divorce rate, and one of the striking differences between divorce today and divorce, say, fifty years ago is in the number of children who now are involved.

Whatever the assessment of the quality of contemporary family life, and it is admittedly very difficult to measure marital happiness much less the overall well-being of children, even the severest critics of the traditional family would hold that as a social institution the family today is less permanent, less stable, and less the social center of life. People are not bound to families as they once were, and the family has become but one of many major institutions in society that shape peoples' lives and to which they hold some allegiance.

## The Neighborhood

One might hope that the decline in household size, the changing character of social relationships, and the family disarray in the metropolitan areas of advanced societies would be compensated for by an increase in the ties of social solidarity within urban neighborhoods. That the single occupant of a household with no family members to turn to, for example, would naturally become more socially intermeshed with the neighbors; and that a decline of allegiance to the family would lead to a growth of allegiance to the larger community. But such is not the case at all. This perspective views various social relationships as functional alternatives to one another, and expects that as individuals lose one set of relationships they will replace them with another set. The fact is, however, that people with large households and strong families tend to neighbor the most, and those with small and weak families neighbor the least. Neighboring and the strength of neighborhood tend to be weakest in situations where there are few families and many single-occupancy households.[41]

It is almost an axiom of urban sociology that urbanization leads to the decline of neighboring and neighborhoods. Strong urban neighborhoods can of course be found in metropolitan settings, but in general neighborhood life is in decline as people turn well beyond the local neighborhood to meet their needs.[42] There are many who argue that nothing is wrong with this; indeed, it further reduces one more ascriptive social tie that, like the family, is not entirely voluntary. After all, why should you be friendly with someone just because they happen to live next door to you? But the capacity to move beyond the neighborhood requires a level of geographic mobility that not everyone possesses. Children do not very often have it, for example, and the quality of neighborhood life becomes very important to them. The elderly do not always have it. And the access to those transportation and communication media necessary to circumvent the neighborhood is typically very limited for the poor, for those in ill health, and for stay-at-home housewives. For all of these people (and if children are included they come close to being a majority of the population) the character of the local neighborhood—whether, for example, friendly or unfriendly—has very real human consequences.

Many of the reasons for the decline of neighborhoods in metropolitan settings have been hinted at above. The neighborhood as a social unit tends to be strongest and neighboring the most active where people have needs that must be met locally, and where neighbors are homogeneous in values and life-style and have lived together for a relatively long period of time. The high rate of residential turnover in cities strongly deters neighboring. So does the population diversity of local areas along age, class, ethnic, or racial lines. And the mobility provided by modern transportation and communication means that many of the daily needs people have can be met well beyond the confines of their proximate environment. Among more affluent metropolitan dwellers, especially, many needs that were once met by neighbors—such as the exchange of goods and services—are now met through the market or outside agencies.

Why bemoan the decline of the neighborhood unit? Because the needs and functions it once served are still highly important. These include mutual aid, sociability and friendship, the socialization of children, and the kind of social control that was discussed above. The significance of the neighborhood is that it is a grouping based on informal contacts, and most of these needs and functions depend heavily on such contacts.[43] It is now well established that in metropolitan areas face-to-face contacts are conducted over a wide geographic range. Social network studies show, for example, that many adults maintain friendships with other adults over long distances.[44] As mentioned above, however, such wide geographic accessibility is not available to everyone.

### Assessing the Effects of Privatization on Personal Well-Being

A sense of personal well-being is strongly related to the material conditions of life—whether one is in good health, is employed, has a satisfactory material standard of living, and so on. Yet the material constitutes only one of several areas of human need, and not necessarily the most important. Following a comprehensive study of welfare in Scandinavia, the Finnish sociologist Eric Allardt noted: "It is hard to avoid the conclusion that the expressions of satisfaction and dissatisfaction only to a very small degree are directly related to the external [material] conditions."[45] One might of course expect such a finding in societies that are both affluent and egalitarian, as are those of Scandinavia. Yet even in the relatively egalitarian United States, a national survey of sense of well-being conducted by the late Angus Campbell found that the contrasts in well-being among people whose patterns of social relationships differ are much sharper than between high-income and low-income people, or among people of differing occupational and educational statuses.[46]

In a widely used conceptual scheme, Eric Allardt has postulated three primary human needs: to have, to relate, and to be.[47] *To have* refers to the material need. *To relate* and *to be* may be rephrased as: *the need to belong socially*, to be attached to others who are significant for one's life; and *the need for a strong and stable cultural identity*, to be "plugged into" a system of values and meanings where one cognitively feels "at home."[48] Belonging may be thought of as more emotional, identity as more mental, but both needs must be fulfilled if an individual is to feel contented, secure, purposeful, and the other attributes that are associated with a strong sense of well-being. In the following discussion, the privatized life in metropolitan communities is examined in terms of both the social relationships that people have and the cultural ties they hold, apart from the material conditions of their lives.

Based on empirical investigations as well as his own clinical practice, Harvard sociologist Robert Weiss has isolated four functions of social relationships that are necessary for our personal well-being.[49] The first is intimacy: we must be able to express our intimate feelings freely and without self-consciousness. To do so, we must have some social relationships that are heavily steeped in trust and effective understanding and with people to whom we have ready access. Relations of intimacy are most commonly held with a marital spouse, a very close relative, or best friend, usually a peer. Persons who lack such intimate relatonships have been shown to be especially low in sense of well-being; such emotional isolation and loneliness has a definite cost in mental health.

A second necessary function of social relationships is social integration. It is important for us to participate with others who share our concerns, others with whom we share experiences, information, and ideas, so that we can feel a part of ongoing life around us. The most common source of relationships for this purpose is our place of work, but those who hold no regular job may turn to neighbors, relatives, or friends from other walks of life. Not to be socially integrated through others is to feel isolated, bored, and lacking in motivation and interest.

A third function of social relationships is the reassurance of our worth, the provision of a sense that we are competent in our main life roles. Again, work is a major source of such relationships. Not to be reassured of our worth is to have a low self-esteem, a feeling that we do not count for much.

The final function of social relationships is to provide assistance and help in meeting life's problems. This can take the form of a service, such as assisting with the care of another's children, or making available resources, such as a rake or the proverbial cup of sugar, or providing reliable knowledge. A main source of such relationships is members of our kin group, but many people also rely heavily on neighbors and other friends. To lack such assistance and help is to feel vulnerable and anxious.

These are the kinds of social relationships, then, that are instrumental in fostering our sense of well-being. Without them, we may fall prey to a range of psychological pathologies, and in the extreme we can become incapacitated with anxiety, depression, and more serious mental breakdown. As noted earlier, the average, well-adjusted person in the metropolitan community maintains these relationships through a far-flung and loose-knit social network of friends, many of whom may not know each other, who have been collected together to serve the various functions. A high percentage of the members of this network are nonrelatives who have been voluntarily chosen for special purposes: a few intimates, some associates to provide social integration and the reassurance of worth, and a few of these who can provide various forms of assistance and help.

For most metropolitan dwellers, these private social networks seemingly function quite well. People must constantly work at maintaining their networks—they cannot readily fall back on such natural, involuntary groupings as kin or neighbors—but they prefer it that way. They prefer being able to choose their own friends and associates rather than having to accept those who biologically or geographically have been thrust upon them. Although there is no way of knowing this for sure, presumably such selectivity and specialization also leads to more satisfactory relationships.

Yet there is one serious problem in all of this: not every metropolitan dweller is adept at making and maintaining a large network of friends. Many lack the social skills, the geographic mobility, or the resources necessary for this purpose. Unlike in the large extended family, or in the solidary and active neighborhood, where life is mainly organized in terms of private social networks, a great many people—those who for one reason or another are unable to form such networks—are left out. They may be the elderly, the handicapped, the poor, the trapped housewife, children, or simply the socially inept. But the fact is that life is not organized in such a way that they are included, and they become in a literal sense social outcasts.

Metropolitan communities are of course not unaware of this problem and there has become established an elaborate set of institutions to serve the socially dispossessed. There are psychologists and psychiatrists for intimacy, hobby clubs for social integration, welfare offices for aid and assistance, singles groups to encourage the formation of new networks, and telephone "hot lines" for an amazingly wide variety of personal problems. In the United States, churches function very powerfully to put people in touch with others and to provide surrogate social relationships when necessary, and thus are a most significant social force in many communities. But at the same time that these outside institutions are helping to pick up the pieces, they may also be exacerbating the problem. As people come to rely more on formal services and less on informal networks, these networks themselves wither still further.[50] We can tell people to go see a psychiatrist rather than spend time with them listening to their intimate feelings; can send them to a welfare office rather than lend them money; and can refer them to a voluntary association rather than participate with them in some common effort. In each instance, the basis for a lasting social relationship is undermined.

The Swedish case is particularly instructive in understanding loneliness and social isolation in metropolitan areas.[51] Although conclusive and generalizable data about the problem do not exist, few Swedes would challenge the proposition that loneliness is a real problem in Swedish metropolitan areas. Moreover, the proposition is held also by most foreign visitors who reside in Sweden for any period of time. A relatively large number of Swedes appear to lack some of the relationships necessary for informal assistance and help, and perhaps for several of the other main functions as well, such as intimacy and social integration.

We have described in previous chapters the life of Swedish metropolitan apartment dwellers, with very low levels of neighboring compounded by small family and household sizes. Although Sweden does have a well-established system of voluntary organizations, the virtual absence of church and other religious ties sets Sweden apart from this aspect of the American local scene; there is nothing in Swedish communities that socially quite takes the place of these absent religious ties. And because residents come to depend informally still less on neighbors and others for assistance and aid, the availability of public services, despite their very positive value on other counts, helps further to isolate Swedes from one another on a daily basis. Finally, contributing to the lack of neighboring, and thus to loneliness, is the excessive formality of traditional Swedish culture, together with the Swedish character trait of emotional restraint and reserve.[52] The story is told of two Danes, two Norwegians, and two Swedes, who are stranded on a desert island. What does each group do? The Danes form a cooperative, the Norwegians start a fight, and the Swedes wait to be introduced! In a society where people need an introduction, informal socializing is often a scarce commodity.

For all these reasons, then, the privatization of many metropolitan Swedes, in its extreme form of loneliness and social isolation, has become a noticeable problem. For those who live alone (now more than a quarter of all Swedes) and who also lack the skills at forming lasting friendships, daily life has become socially cut off despite being surrounded physically by thousands of people. It is, as Louis Wirth once noted, a life marked by physical proximity but social distance. That so many Swedes long to return to the small, traditional communities that until only very recently dominated Swedish society is little wonder.

Loneliness and social isolation do not seem to be problems of the same magnitude in metropolitan United States (and still less so in Britain).

American family and household sizes are larger than those of Sweden, thus providing more candidates for social relationships. Americans can still rely on their neighbors more than Swedes are able to. This is partly due to the lower densities of American residential development, partly to the greater need for mutual aid and assistance in American life because of the lack of public services, and partly to the fact that Americans, all of whom at some point in their genealogy were strangers in a foreign land, have a greater knack for informal socializing with others. Finally, many Americans have strong church ties, as mentioned above, which often function to provide important social connections.

Loneliness and social isolation are by no means absent in American metropolitan life, however; indeed, they appear to be growing as real social issues.[53] The United States may lag slightly behind Sweden in several of the social trends noted above, such as declining family and household size and weaker neighboring, but the social direction seems clear. Moreover, there are two social conditions that promote these problems to a degree not found in Sweden. The constant residential mobility of a very transient society clearly takes its toll on social relationships. And the high crime rate breeds a mistrust among people, plus a propensity to "stay indoors" and out of the way of others, that seriously dampens the social relationships necessary for our sense of well-being. It may also be the case that family instability and the instability of social relationships in general is greater in American life, although reliable comparative data on this are not available.

If social attachment is a somewhat less serious problem in the United States than it is in Sweden, cultural attachment is a more serious one. The quintessential personal problem in many American metropolitan areas may be the lack of strong cultural identity—a deficiency in the degree to which Americans feel plugged into an integrated world of values and meanings where they cognitively can feel at home. Put in classic sociological terms, this is a condition of anomie—when values and meanings are conflicting, weak, or absent.

Culture is to human beings as water is to a fish—because it is all around us, all the time, its importance may go unrecognized. Surely it is awkward at best to ask the average person about his or her problems of cultural meaning; the concept is too vague and abstract. And it is difficult to assay precisely what follows from a condition of anomie. Mental anxiety together with feelings of vulnerability at the very least. But what else? Nevertheless the problem, once stated, should be recognizable to most readers.

Culture for human beings fulfills some of the same functions that instincts do for lower animals. It guides behavior in certain directions and thereby limits the making of choices. In modern societies the issue of maximizing personal choice has become almost a sacred tenet; we all want to be able to decide for ourselves. But most of our daily behaviors—how we greet people, how we act toward our children, how we behave in the company of strangers—are dictated by the force of custom, and fortunate it is that is so, for we would be virtually paralyzed into inactivity if we had to stop, think, and consciously decide before each pattern of action. A problem comes when we receive conflicting messages, when the force of custom becomes the force of many different customs; some say do one thing, and some say do another.

All modern societies are filled with such conflicting cultural messages: Should I be especially protective toward women or treat them more as equals; favor my own self-satisfaction or the value of marital fidelity; be neighborly and do my neighbor a favor or mind my own business; contribute to society through having and raising children or single-mindedly advance my career. Such conflicts among cultural norms stem largely from rapid social change. With women now heavily in the work force, for example, the cultural norms that define gender roles must change. But they change erratically and unevenly. Conflicting cultural messages also are caused by many different cultural traditions coalescing in one society, as is the case especially in the United States.

Sweden has something of a cultural advantage due to homogeneity. While it has faced very rapid social change, the society has remained relatively homogeneous in ethnic makeup with a still largely intact national culture. The influx of foreign workers since World War II is changing this situation today, but the average Swede still feels closely tied—and united with others in being so—to a national culture with a few clear central meanings. Whatever cultural contradictions there are at the metropolitan level (and intersocietal differences are not too great in this regard) these are partly compensated for by high national cultural solidarity.

In the United States the cultural climate is very dissimilar. A product of both rapid social change and strong ethnic and racial heterogeneity, the nation as a whole may have what is the least integrated culture among the advanced societies. To some observers this is masked by an overlay of patriotism. The flag, "The Star Spangled Banner," and "In God We Trust" give an aura of cultural solidarity, but such patriotism does not carry very far into daily life. Americans may have a strong allegiance to their national society, but the cultural meanings and values that guide their lives come more from local groupings, whether those groupings are autonomous religious bodies, ethnic or racial ghettos, or traditional communities.[54]

It is precisely because of the American reliance on local cultural groupings that the privatization of life in metropolitan areas has such a marked impact on the cultural sphere. As these local cultural groupings break down and are replaced by the more privatized sociocultural networks, the chances for cultural anomie increase dramatically. Each social network can become a cultural world of its own making, with residential environments consisting of a bewildering variety of such private cultural worlds. This may add up to a cultural scene that is exciting, even exhilarating, and it is surely a stimulus to cultural innovation. But beyond a certain point it can be very unsettling, and lead to moral anxiety and aimlessness.

At the extreme, people's social networks develop individualized cultural spheres that are lacking in public attachments; as private subcultures they have no institutional supports from the larger community. The lack of continuing public legitimation is a main source of "weak" values and meanings, and the effect is similar to values being in contradiction: high personal anxiety because society no longer has the feel of a cognitively comfortable and secure place.

Moreover, there is again the problem of the unattached, the person who for a variety of reasons is unable to link up in a satisfactory way with a private social and cultural network and is forced to face life at the mercy of what has been called the "mass society."[55] Bereft of both private networks and traditional groupings, the dominant force in this person's life becomes the mass media, especially television, and whatever meanings and values these media impart. Far from maximizing human choice, this situation represents an apogee of cultural coercion in which the citizen is every bit as much a puppet as under a doctrinaire political totalitarianism.

In summary, metropolitan life is split between formal connections, such as work and relations with government authorities, and private connections, the the latter providing at their best bastions of intimacy and identity for individuals apart from the outside world. But not every individual is so protected, and the private bastions themselves are vulnerable to instability and breakdown. Certain forms of social attachment can become tenuous, best seen in the Swedish case, and cultural attachments can become ambiguous, best viewed in the American case. Each stems in part from excessive privatization, and the two combined add up to a sociocultural climate in which the contacts among people are cold, uncertain and nonsupportive, and the values and meanings are weak and contradictory. When this happens, people are thrown on the mercy of mass society, and what a far cry that is from the human ennoblement that was privatism's original promise.

## Notes

1. Hannah Arendt, *The Human Condition* (Garden City, NY: Doubleday/Anchor, 1959), p.53.
2. Ibid., p. 48.
3. See, for example, Peter Berger, B. Berger, and H. Kellner *The Homeless Mind*

(New York: Random House, 1973); Arthur Brittan, *The Privatized World* (London: Routledge & Kegan Paul, 1977); and Joseph Bensman and Robert Lilienfeld, *Between Public and Private* (New York: Free Press, 1979). One exception, which emphasizes urban life, is Richard Sennett, *The Fall of Public Man* (New York: Knopf, 1977).

4. Definitions from *The Random House Dictionary of the English Language* (New York: Random House, 1968).
5. See, for example, National Institute of Mental Health, *Television and Behavior: Ten Years of Scientific Progress and Implications for the Eighties* (Washington, DC: Government Printing Office, 1982).
6. Robert Sommer, J. Herrick, and T. Sommer, "The Behavioral Ecology of Supermarkets and Farmers' Markets," *Journal of Environmental Psychology* 1 (1981): 13-19.
7. Louis Wirth, "Urbanism as a Way of Life" in *Neighborhood, City and Metropolis*, ed. R. Gutman and D. Popenoe (New York: Random House, 1970), pp. 54-69.
8. An excellent review of research inspired by Wirth is R.N. Morris, *Urban Sociology* (New York: Praeger, 1968).
9. For an influential recent statement, see Stanley Milgram, "The Experience of Living in Cities," *Science* 167 (March 1970): 1461-69.
10. Claude S. Fischer, "The Public and Private Worlds of City Life," *American Sociological Review* 46 (June 1981): 306-16.
11. M.E. Wolfgang, "Urban Crime," in *The Metropolitan Enigma*, ed., J.Q. Wilson (New York: Doubleday/Anchor, 1970), pp. 270-311.
12. Sam Bass Warner, Jr., *The Private City* (Philadelphia: University of Pennsylvania Press, 1968).
13. Ibid., pp. 10-11.
14. Ibid., p. 21.
15. Berger et al., *Homeless Mind*, ch. 3.
16. See Elizabeth Bott, *Family and Social Network*, 2d ed. (London; Tavistock, 1971).
17. Claude S. Fischer, *To Dwell Among Friends* (Chicago: University of Chicago Press, 1982; Claude S. Fischer et al., *Networks and Places* (New York: Free Press. 1977); and Barry Wellman, "The Community Question," *American Journal of Sociology* 84 (March 1979).
18. See Yi-Fu Tuan, *Segmented Worlds and Self* (Minneapolis: University of Minnesota Press, 1982).
19. Lyn Lofland, *A World of Strangers* (New York: Basic Books, 1973). See also Sennett, *Fall of Public Man.*
20. Lofland, *World of Strangers*, p. 82.
21. An excellent review of the research is Albert K. Cohen and James F. Short, Jr., "Crime and Juvenile Delinquency," in *Contemporary Social Problems*, ed. R.K. Merton and R. Nisbet 4th ed. (New York: Harcourt Brace Jovanovich, 1976).
22. An influential statement of social control theory is Travis Hirschi, *Causes of Delinquency* (Berkeley: University of California Press, 1969).
23. For relevant research on this general topic, see Terry L. Baumer, "Research on Fear of Crime in the United States," *Victimology* 3 (1978): 254-364; B.Latane and J.M. Darley *The Unresponsive Bystander* (New York: Appleton-Century-Crofts, 1970); C. Korte, "Helpfulness in the Urban Environment" in *Advances*

*in the Studies of Environment and Behavior,* vol. 1, *The Urban Environment,* ed. A. Baum et al. (Hillsdale, NJ: Erlbaum, 1978); James C. Hackler, Kwai-Yui Ho, and Carol Urquhart Ross, "The Willingness to Intervene: Differing Community Characteristics," *Social Problems* 21 (1974): 328-44; and Albert Hunter and T.L. Baumer, "Street Traffic, Social Integration, and Fear of Crime," *Sociological Inquiry* 152 (Spring 1982): 122-31.

24. Arendt, *Human Condition* p. 55.
25. Christopher Lasch, *The Culture of Narcissim* (New York: Norton, 1978), p. 27.
26. Definition is that used by the U.S. Census.
27. Diana De Are and L. Long, "Meet the Average American," *American Demograhics,* April 1981, p. 23.
28. Editors of Heron House, *The Book of Numbers* (New York: A & W Publishers, 1978), p. 143; *Statistical Abstract of Sweden, 1984* (Stockholm: Central Statistical Bureau, 1984), p. 39.
29. Robert T. Michael et al., "Changes in the Propensity to Live Alone," *Demography* 17 (February 1980): 39-56.
30. *World Population Data Sheet* (Washington, DC, Population Reference Bureau, 1982).
31. Michael et al., "Changes in the Propensity to Live Alone."
32. George Masnick and M.J. Bane, *The Nation's Families: 1960-1990* (Cambridge, MA: Joint Center for Urban Studies, 1980), ch. 2.
33. Peter Laslett, *Family Life and Illicit Love in Earlier Generations* (New York: Cambridge University Press, 1977), ch. 1.
34. Masnick and Bane, *Nation's Families.*
35. Those who can afford it have been able to maintain communication through the media of mass communication and transportation, however. See, Bert N. Adams, *Kinship in an Urban Setting* (Chicago: Markham, 1968); and Sheila Klatzky, *Patterns of Contact with Relatives* (Washington, DC: American Sociological Association, 1974).
36. The originator of the concept "isolated nuclear family" was Talcott Parsons in "The Kinship System of the Contemporary United States," *Essays in Sociological Theory* (Glencoe, Ill. Free Press, 1954). In its extreme form, the trend toward the isolated nuclear family has been questioned through such historical analyses as Michael Anderson, *Family Structure in Nineteenth Century Lancashire* (London: Cambridge University Press, 1971); and Michael B. Katz, *The People of Hamilton, Canada West: Family and Class in Mid-Nineteenth Century City* (Cambridge: Harvard University Press, 1975). Such analyses have found more connections among relatives in urban settings than one might have expected, but that there is a long-term trend toward the isolation of the nuclear family from other relatives nonetheless seems unmistakable.
37. The distinction is widely discussed in anthropological literature. For a contemporary discussion, as well as empirical analysis, see Graham A. Allan, *A Sociology of Friendship and Kinship* (Boston: Allen & Unwin, 1979).
38. Robert R. Bell, *Worlds of Friendship* (Beverly Hills: Sage 1981).
39. See, for example, Fischer, *To Dwell Among Friends*; and Fischer et al., *Networks and Places.*
40. See Bernikow, Louise, "Alone: Yearning for Companionship in America," *New York Times Magazine,* August 15, 1982, pp. 24ff.
41. See Suzanne Keller, *The Urban Neighborhood* (New York: Random House, 1968); and Fischer, *To Dwell Among Friends.*

42. See Donald I. Warren, *Helping Networks* (Notre Dame: University of Notre Dame Press, 1981).
43. Albert Hunter, "The Urban Neighborhood: Its Analytical and Social Contexts," *Urban Affairs Quarterly* 14 (1979): 267-88.
44. Wellman, "Community Question"; and Fischer, *To Dwell Among Friends.*
45. Quoted in Angus Campbell, *The Sense of Well-Being in America* (New York: McGraw-Hill, 1981), p. 230.
46. Ibid.
47. Eric Allardt, "Dimension of Welfare in a Comparative Scandinavian Study," *Acta Sociologica* 19 (1976): 227-39.
48. See Berger et al., *Homeless Mind.*
49. Robert S. Weiss, "The Fund of Sociability," *Transaction/Society*, July-August 1969.
50. This is a main thesis of Christopher Lasch, *Haven in a Heartless World* (New York: Basic Books, 1977).
51. This is explored in David Popenoe, *The Suburban Environment: Sweden and the United States* (Chicago: University of Chicago Press, 1977).
52. See Paul Britten Austin, *On Being Swedish* (Coral Gables: University of Miami Press, 1968).
53. See Bernikow, "Alone"; and Robert S. Weiss, *Loneliness: The Experience of Emotional and Social Isolation* (Cambridge: MIT Press, 1973).
54. See Robert H. Wiebe, *The Segmented Society* (New York: Oxford University Press, 1975).
55. W. Kornhauser, *The Politics of Mass Society* (New York: Free Press, 1959); and "Mass Society" in *International Encyclopedia of the Social Sciences*, ed. D.L. Sills (New York: Macmillan, 1968).

# 8

# Changing the Metropolitan Community in the United States

If the argument put forth in the last chapter has validity, that a major problem in metropolitan communities is the excessive privatization of life, we must look for ways to bring to modern residential living a greater measure of publicness. We must seek to strengthen those ties that bind people in local areas to one another, and that loosen the grip of privatism. There are obviously no easy answers to a process so entrenched as the privatization of contemporary metropolitan life, and I do not pretend to be able to provide any. I would feel remiss, nevertheless, and this book would not seem complete, without some discussion of "solutions." In this final chapter, by putting forth some guidelines for metropolitan community development, I hope at least to stimulate ways of thinking about future metropolitan development that may in themselves help to promote needed social change.

I will limit my discussion of guidelines to the American scene. It would be nice to be able to proffer some "solutions" for Europe as well, but I will resist the temptation to do so. Unlike the detached social scientific analysis of conditions, the framing of practical and realistic public policy guidelines requires a level of political sophistication that is difficult for a foreigner to a society fully to achieve. I, at least, feel much more comfortable in this regard when I stay close to home.

Before turning to these guidelines, let us put the current metropolitan situation in perspective by examining some metropolitan trends and alternatives.

## The End of Metropolitan Growth

In each society in the last few decades there has occurred for the first time since the industrial revolution what appears to be the end of metropolitan growth. In the United States during the 1970s, for example, non-metropolitan counties grew faster than metropolitan counties. In the case of several of the larger and older metropolitan areas, there was an absolute decline in population size for the first time in American history. This resulted from declining birth rates within metropolitan areas, people's moving into fringe areas that are not officially classified as part of the metropolis but from which residents still commute to metropolitan jobs, and people's leaving the larger metropolitan regions entirely in search of jobs and a better life in smaller places.[1]

The main focus of attention has been on the latter group of people, and a variety of push and pull factors is associated with their move. For many, the movement of industrial jobs has triggered their residential mobility. Others, such as the growing body of elderly persons living on transfer payments, no longer need an attachment to centers of employment. Still others flee the large cities to escape crime and what is regarded to be an overcrowded environment. Whatever the reasons, their new lives are enhanced by the media of mass transportation and communication that have diminished the traditional parochialism of small places, and that at the same time have made those places more accessible to the facilities and services of metropolitan centers. The automobile, the telephone, the computer, the television set, the interstate highway system, and the jet airplane all play a seminal role in permitting a more decentralized yet still relatively urbane community life, one in which strong ties to a national and even world culture can be continued and quality services in health care and education are within reach.

In view of this trend, could it be said that the United States is undergoing a process of demetropolitanization? Because the smaller and more recently developed metropolitan areas continue to expand and entirely new metropolitan areas are being formed by the influx of population into nonmetropolitan places, the percentage of the U.S. population living in metropolitan communities has remained constant: about 75 percent. Thus, *demetropolitanization* is not the correct term for what is happening. The great bulk of the population still will be living within the confines of metropolitan areas in the foreseeable future. It can be said with certainty, however, that the era of metropolitanism has reached a plateau, and that there is now a tendency for people to live in smaller-scale residential environments.

What was triggered mainly by market forces in the United States (although aided by federal assistance through the development of interstate highways and nonmetropolitan defense industries, and by federal income-transfer payments) has been for several decades a major goal of government planning in the other nations. Active Swedish government efforts at industrial decentralization (providing subsidies for industries to locate in remote areas, for example) and the British New Towns program (which during the period 1945-70 constructed about 4 percent of British housing units)[2] have fostered a population trend similar to that in the United States. In these nations, too, the population growth of larger metropolitan areas has been halted and people increasingly are living in smaller places.

## Scale and the Quality of Community Life

Any decentralization that takes place brings the scale of the communities in which people live more in line with their personal preferences. In general, people much prefer smaller places. A study conducted for the U.S. Commission on Population Growth and the American Future, for example, showed that 34 percent of Americans would prefer to live in open country; 30 percent, in small town or city; 22 percent, in medium-sized city or suburb; and only 14 percent, in larger city or suburb.[3]

The subjective reality that lies behind these preferences was turned up by Angus Campbell's national surveys of peoples' sense of well-being. He found that "the larger the community a person lives in, the less likely he or she is to say that it is 'a good place to live.'"[4] The residents of larger places are especially dissatisfied with the schools, high taxes, crime, and general environmental conditions. Also, "the larger the community in which people live, the less likely they are to be fully satisfied with their immediate neighborhood"[5] (although people tend to be more satisfied with their neighborhoods than with their communities). The people most contented with their residential environments, according to Campbell, are those living in rural areas—counties that have no town as large as 50,000; towns smaller than 2,500; and open country. Such people "are much more likely to socialize with their neighbors, they are far less concerned with pollution, and they are much freer of fear of crime. They are also generally more satisfied with their lives."[6]

Are people's subjective preferences for smaller places backed up by any objective data that such places really have an improved quality of life? At least for urban areas in the United States, there are firm statistical correlations between smaller-sized communities and reductions in crime, traffic congestion and associated death rates from automobile accidents, and air pollution.[7] But the correlations are not strong either in absolute or relative terms.[8] A person moving from a large central city to a rural area might be expected to find significant improvements in the quality of life along several important dimensions. But a person moving, say, from a metropolis of 500,000 to one of 100,000, would probably not find substantial differences, and any improvements would most likely be due to factors other than sheer size of community, such as population makeup, economic opportunity, and housing. In a Swedish comparison between two very similar residential districts of apartment dwellers, one in Stockholm and the other in a Swedish community of 50,000-75,000 people, I found that the actual social differences in people's lives were not very large. The degree of publicness, at least for the apartment dwellers, was not substantially greater in the smaller town.[9] Based on the findings we have to date, then, one may conclude that the modest decentralization of the population currently under way in advanced societies will not in itself lead to a significant change in the quality of community life, although it will likely make some contribution to that end.

## Metropolitan Alternatives

If decentralization were to be carried out more extensively, of course, the contribution would be greater. Utopians have long proposed a mass movement back to small communities, a kind of democratic exodus from urban places.[10] But short of some kind of national crisis, radical decentralization in advanced societies seems out of the question. The scarcity of land, steep increases in transport distances, and the necessity of duplicating already existing public facilities would make it enormously expensive. And the press of higher priorities would rule it out in any event from an economic standpoint.

Such radical decentralization was clearly one of the main goals of the post–World War II New Towns program in Great Britain, wherein some thirty new towns were launched between 1946 and 1970, several having target populations of over 200,000 people.[11] The program has met with reasonable success, but that success has been more in demonstrating sound principles of town planning than in bringing a sizable portion of the British population to improved communities of a modest scale.[12] And the British now realize what they probably should have known at the beginning: why build entirely new towns on virgin land (or more typically prime agricultural land) when you could use the same money to improve an old town. Thus what is called the expanded towns program has come to replace the new towns program, albeit on a much diminished scale: the goals in building a new town are essentially achieved while at the same time an old town is being salvaged and restored. In the United States, a modest new towns program was launched in the late 1960s, but it soon floundered financially and is now virtually dead.

The hard reality is that, despite people's personal preferences to the contrary, there is little hope of modifying in any significant way the dominance of the metropolis in modern life. In scale, the communities of the future in advanced societies are not going to be much different from those now in existence, although the smaller ones may grow faster than they have in the past and the larger ones more slowly, and even decline. It is therefore not the scale but the social structure of existing communities that should command the nation's attention.

## Alternatives to the Private Household?

The privatization of life in metropolitan areas, as we have seen, is a product not only of changing community structure but also the rise of the highly private household. Is there a possibility of modifying this household type in some way?

Modern societies have been host to many social experiments whose goal has been to create a more public life through breaking up the private, separate household. Not long ago the most widely discussed alternative to the privatized household was the commune. During its heyday in the late 1960s, some observers saw in the commune a real hope for the future of modern civilization. At last a way seemingly had been found to reintegrate people with one another based on love and cooperation. Today, such hopes seem a distant relic of a troubled past. The rate of communal breakdown has proved to be far greater than the rate of family breakdown, and while some communes linger on, especially those that are religiously oriented and located in isolated rural areas, most urban communes have long since disintegrated into their constituent parts of lonely and isolated individuals.[13]

The urban communes were doomed from the start. It was too much to expect many individuals raised in highly individualistic and privatized homes suddenly to cast off these socialized tendencies and go to an opposite extreme. More than anything else, the commune was a substitute for the nuclear family, or more precisely the nuclear marriage because few children have ever been involved in communal living. Yet with marriages breaking down in part because people find difficulty intimately adapting to one other person, why should anyone have thought it possible for those same people to be able intimately to adapt to perhaps six or a dozen others? This kind of group adaptation is possible with fellow kin, for reasons mentioned in the last chapter, but seldom historically has it ever been possible among "just friends."

The same fate awaited most of the "collective houses" in the cities of Sweden that have been established over the years. These are typically large apartment buildings in which people continue to live in small private households but share a variety of common facilities, such as those for eating. An identifiable evolutionary pattern has almost always been followed by the Swedish collective houses. After an early period of idealism, people withdraw more and more to their private quarters, especially for food preparation and eating. Eventually the collective eating facilties go out of business and this signals the gradual decline of the collectivity as a whole, leading eventually to an ordinary apartment building mainly for singles (who are best adapted to the small housing units and who benefit most from the few collective services that remain). Again, it appears that even under the most favorable of circumstances people are unable socially to venture far beyond the privatized household in their basic, day-to-day arrangements of life. Nonetheless, Swedes have not stopped experimenting with collective houses; the alternative is still actively discussed and new attempts are occasionally brought into being.

Worth mentioning is another radical communitarian movement in advanced societies that has been very successful on its own terms: the Israeli kibbutzim. But these are rural, not urban, settlements, and even in the highly favorable cultural climate of Israel they encompass only a tiny part of the Israeli population, a part that is getting smaller each year. Moreover, there is now growing evidence that the strong tendency toward household privatism described above is quietly overtaking the kibbutzim. The nuclear families of the kibbutz are increasingly desirous of more private space, a larger role in the raising of their own children, and greater insulation from group activities and even group norms.[14]

One could add that the same tendency toward household privatism can be seen in the communist nations of Eastern Europe. There, housing shortages have forced a level of residential cooperation and an extended familism from which urban residents are seeking to rebel, and one of the most coveted of life's goals is to have an apartment of one's own.

From these international examples it surely is reasonable to conclude that radical alternatives to the private and separate household are not likely short of a massive shift in both culture and personality. The human products of many centuries of Western civilization seem to demand, and postindustrial culture appears to dictate, a very large measure of privatization and independence for individuals. The issue, therefore, is not to discover an alternative to the private household. It is to find ways of redressing the balance between household and community; to retain a measure of privacy while at the same time building stronger public attitudes and connections through which people will be able to find more social attachments and meaning and communities will more successfully be able to function. And these ways must be applicable to the residential environment where most people will continue to live: the metropolitan area.

## Guidelines for American Metropolitan Community Development

Attention has long focused on ways of improving the management of metropolitan areas as a whole. Surely, in view of the European experience, they can be better governed and more efficiently ordered than is the case today, despite the great aversion in the United States to metropolitan government. But no matter how well governed or planned, the metropolis as a whole remains a megacommunity whose dimensions far exceed the human scale of everyday living. The most important concern of metropolitan community development, therefore, should be the constituent subcommunities that make up the metropolis. Urban life historically has consisted of a medley of "urban villages," and the American metropolitan community is a legacy of this tradition. But these subcommunities, if they are not to be washed away in an urban tide, must be preserved, protected, and encouraged to function and grow.

The guidelines to follow are directed toward this end. They emphasize physical development, for that is a realm, as we know from the European experience, in which public action can have a marked effect. Some of these guidelines may be obvious, none is novel, and most require public actions that politically would not be easy to achieve. Yet each posits a goal for which we must strive if we are to make any dent in the private drift of American metropolitan life.

### Residential Stability

Studies show that length of time spent in a community is the best predictor of community attachments: the longer one lives in a community, the more publicly attached to it one becomes.[15] Although our rate of residential mobility has been gradually dropping in recent years, American communities are still probably the most mobile in the world.[16] It is essential that the rate of residential mobility be lowered still further.

People move for two main reasons: housing and jobs. Housing moves typically are the automatic accompaniment of going through the life cycle—leaving the parents' home, marriage, children, retirement. As people's needs for space change, they move to housing of a different type. Job moves usually stem from the desire to upgrade employment, or from economic fluctuations and the loss of employment. In both housing and job moves it is important to minimize the necessity that a person has to leave a community entirely. This requires that each local community have a relatively large and diverse job market, and a diverse housing market.

The goal of a large and diverse job market means that "balanced" local economies should be promoted over those that are highly specialized; it is a goal that is as commonly held as it is difficult to achieve. The goal of a diversified housing stock in local areas, in contrast, is easier to achieve but less widely accepted. It contradicts the American penchant, especially in suburban areas, for large-scale homogeneous communities.

In common practice, suburban zoning ordinances restrict housing to a very limited number of sizes and price ranges, and thereby generate much needless residential mobility. Community residents who merely need housing of a type different from that provided locally (this typically includes most of the community's sons and daughters at some time in their lives) must leave the area to get it. The problem of local housing homogeneity has been partially corrected by recent market forces, which have generated a striking increase in smaller units, especially in garden apartment complexes, at the expense of the single-family house. Nevertheless, there is much more that most local communities could do in this regard.

## Functional Balance

Metropolitan conditions, especially in the United States as discussed in previous chapters, have fostered great functional specialization of local areas. One area will have the workplaces, another the shopping, and a third the residences. A social consequence of this is that there is little overlap in the social attachments made in the three districts: As workers go off to their far-flung homes at the end of the day, friends made at work are left behind; neighbors are seldom co-workers; and the shopping areas are depersonalized, with a familiar face seldom to be seen. Friendships in metropolitan settings are fragile enough without these kinds of impediments. The reestablishment of more functional balance in metropolitan local areas, therefore, could enhance the formation of "tightly knit" social networks, that is, networks in which the participants know and relate to one another rather than just to the person around whom the network is formed.

Greater functional balance could also cut the length of the journey to work, and thus diminish essentially wasted time that could with social profit be spent on family, neighborhood, and other forms of social interaction. In the larger metropolitan areas, where places of work can be very far from people's residences, the long journey to work can be a significant impediment to a rich community life. In writing or revising local zoning ordinances, such considerations should be kept more in the forefront.

## Political and Social Autonomy

The autonomous and self-sufficient community, one that subsists on and controls its own economic, political, and social life, is a creature of the very distant historical past. Every community in advanced societies, from small town to large metropolis, is heavily dependent on the outside world—other communities and the national society—for economic goods and services, for political decisions, and for social and cultural inputs.[17] Yet it is possible for many communities to be more autonomous than they are now in ways that can make a significant difference in the residents' lives.

Why is increased local community autonomy such an important goal? Because there needs to be a strong public buffer between citizen and society, a set of "mediating structures" that serves as a vehicle for social interaction and provides some insulation and repose from the contradictory and amorphous demands of mass society.[18]

Emile Durkheim felt that occupational groups, such as professional associations, would emerge as such a buffer, but the very specialized nature of these groups in advanced societies appears to preclude their use for that purpose.[19] In Sweden and even more in Japan the work organization plays this role in a significant way. But it is hard to foresee that the American work organization could take on this additional social task without a radical change of spirit and operation. Religion plays this role in the United States; it is extremely important for some but not for the majority. This leaves the local community, whose autonomy in political and social terms can be strengthened in various ways even if economic self-sufficiency no longer is either a possible or desirable goal.

The political and social dimensions of the local community are closely interrelated. Community political action, the capacity of local citizens to confront their own problems with concerted activity that involves the wide participation of residents, is naturally greater in communities where members feel that they really belong together and share a common life. And community political action, in turn, can deepen community social solidarity. One important way to promote political action in local communities is to create greater congruence between economic and especially political and social boundaries. As discussed in chapter 6, metropolitan life in the United States is characterized by social communities whose political outlets are highly fractionated among different towns, counties, and other political units, and by political jurisdictions that may have little social unity to back them up. Following the European lead, the United States should make a much greater effort to achieve a rearrangement of local government jurisdictions around viable social entities.

The social attachment people feel toward their communities can probably be intensified through physical design. Communities should have strong physical boundaries, as is provided by green belts for example, so that it is immediately clear who is, and who is not, a community member. And communities should have strong focal points, such as a distinct city center, to help generate a more centripetal orientation.[20] In the newer metropolitan areas of North America especially, with their endless urban sprawl, such physical attributes are in very short supply.[21] A practice that has been severely curtailed in Europe, the building of outlying shopping centers, can be particularly destructive of community life.

Probably the most important single vehicle for the advancement of community political and social autonomy is a local newspaper.[22] Without this, a community's chances for a measure of solidarity and collective action are slim indeed. Such local newspapers should be given public financial support when necessary to keep them going, as they are in many European countries. Also necessary is the provision of a variety of public facilities and services.

## Social and Cultural Facilities

Americans are very fond of building housing projects; we take great pride in being a nation well housed. What too often are overlooked (because they usually require public, not private, expenditures) are those cultural and social facilities that help to turn a mere housing project into a community. The United States has been outstanding in building public schools, but beyond that many communities are seriously deficient, by European standards, in facilities and services for recreation, welfare, child care, youth, and the elderly. The tradition of family self-sufficiency has helped to curtail these important community elements, but with family breakdown and the rapid growth of highly dependent small households, the lack of community facilities is a social drawback of no mean proportions. Of all the strategies discussed in this chapter, this is one of the easiest to implement, requiring as it does only a modest change of political priorities in public expenditures.

Community facilities—parks and playgrounds, day care centers, youth centers, centers for the elderly—make their own direct contribution to the reduction of poverty and delinquency, and to the health and happiness of community members. But they also provide additional channels for community participation, vehicles through which social interaction is generated and community solidarity promoted. The community with few public facilities should not wonder for long why its citizens are living in a myriad of diverse outside worlds, why they have little local interest, and why they effortlessly drift away.

## Neighborhood Homogeneity and Community Diversity

This is one of the most controversial areas in American community life. That people feel more at ease, make more friends, and have more public connections when they live with others who are close to themselves in class level, ethnicity and race, age, and stage of the life cycle is a sociological axiom. For this reason, and where the market permits as it does in U.S. metropolitan areas, a tremendous amount of residential clustering occurs, the clusters consisting of people who are highly homogeneous with one another. We see this dramatically in the exclusive upper-middle-class family suburbs, in the new communities for the elderly, in the center-city gay areas, and in the ethnic and racial ghettos. In the latter case, of course, the residents are only partly clustered by choice and partly by force of discrimination, and they must take locations that are left over after spatial decisions have been made by those with more power and other resources.

The typical conservative impulse calls for accentuating the "natural" social clustering that already occurs. It mandates not only homogeneous neighborhoods within communities, but homogeneous communities as a whole, with the end result being a patchwork quilt of communities that would be even more markedly distinguishable from one another in terms of social class, life-cycle stage, and race and ethnicity than they are today. There are very sound sociological as well as practical reasons for not following this impulse, however. Such massive community homogenization would in the first instance violate several of the community development guidelines that have already been noted. The greater separation of life-cycle stages, for example, would lead to even more residential instability than we have now, as people were forced to move around from community to community as they grew older. And an increase in class segregation would compromise the goal of functional balance, which demands a relatively high level of community diversity in this regard because of the wide range of occupations that are involved.

But a broader issue is this: communities that are highly differentiated from each other tend to generate a high level of political conflict because they are in a constant, long-range struggle over securing their special share of society's resources. Differentiated communities demand very different kinds of resources: schools for some, health care for others, job programs for still others, and so on. Intracommunity conflicts over the division of scarce resources can be sharp enough. As these conflicts are extended over longer distances, at higher levels of government, and among people who in few other instances have any occasion to communicate with one another, the degree of political and social virulence can escalate significantly. The many center city-suburban political battles in the United States are examples of this.

A nation as large and diverse as the United States desperately needs local political buffers to help diffuse such intergroup animosities. Ideally, each local community should be an approximate microcosm of the demographic makeup of the nation as a whole. That way the scramble for resources would take place, at least in the first round, among people who see one another on a daily basis in a variety of capacities, who share some common life together, and who must continue living with one another after the resources have been allocated.

There are many other reasons, some more subtle, why highly homogeneous local communities are undesirable. They can be boring and even stultifying; human diversity is a powerful stimulus for creative human endeavors of all kinds. The further geographic separation of the lower classes would work seriously to the disadvantage of these classes, cutting off chances for upward social mobility and draining their communities of middle-class leadership. And increased geographic separation of people by life stage would curtail still more that intangible sense of the wholeness of life, from birth to death, that already has become so feeble in modern societies.

How, then, is one to have heterogeneous communities yet at the same time preserve the real social advantages that accrue from homogeneous clustering? The answer is to promote homogeneous neighborhoods, but only up to a certain size limit. Contrary to the views of some, who favor the substantial residential intermixing of peoples in pursuit of what they feel would be greater equality, the community considerations that are the focus of this book suggest a high level of neighborhood homogeneity.[23] There is no good reason, in my opinion, that people should not be permitted to have living near them others with whom they feel comfortable, whose basic values they share, and who provide the best pool for the formation of friendships. Such neighborhood groupings, moreover, should be protected through public powers. It matters not whether the groupings are single class, life-style, age, ethnic group, or race—each is a category in terms of which people may have a natural affinity, and this natural affinity should be preserved and enhanced at any reasonable cost.

But a firm line must be drawn to prevent these clusterings from becoming so large that their members are insulated from the larger community. It is not clear precisely what the upper limit in size should be; it undoubtedly varies from situation to situation, group to group. Some have suggested clusterings of several hundred or more households, enough to make up a neighborhood primary school.[24] But there are many good reasons that social integration in the United States should begin at a young age, and this suggests elementary school districts that are quite diverse. It may be that an optimum natural clustering is no more than twenty-five to fifty households. In any event, the size of each grouping should not be so large that the community as a whole is thereby prevented from attaining a large measure of diversity.

The pathologies of metropolitan life seem to escalate with each passing year, and all but the most starry eyed and optimistic are coming to feel that it is time for some change of direction. The religious renaissance, the flight from the city to smaller places, the commune and the counterculture, the popularity of group and even mass psychotherapies and "consciousness raising" all attest a deep-seated desire for social change that can generate more interpersonal connectedness and cultural meaning.

Especially in the United States the search for change turns to the novel and the bizarre. But it is the conclusion of this study that we must look instead at the basic fundamentals of social life. There is a little evidence that realistic social alternatives exist for the traditional structures of family and kin group, neighborhood and community. Although these groups have become truncated and distorted under modern conditions, this does not decrease their importance or suggest that there are better alternatives. Indeed, as I read the evidence, it is all to the contrary. To the degree that family and kin group, neighborhood and community are still viable, the members of these structures tend to be the most satisfied with their lives, and the personal and social pathologies are fewest.

From his surveys in the mid-1970s, Angus Campbell found that many people are coming to share this conclusion: they now place much more importance on "the need for sensitive and responsive martial relationships . . . for the respect and approval of friends, for identification with community."[25] And in a recent study, Daniel Yankelovich detected what he thinks is a sweeping cultural revolution that is transforming the rules of American life and generating "a new social ethic," an "ethic of commitment." He sees two kinds of commitment emerging: forming closer and deeper personal relationships; and trading some instrumental values for sacred/expressive ones. As evidence for the first kind of commitment, he finds that "70 percent of Americans now recognize that while they have many acquaintances, they have few close friends, and they experience this as a serious void in their lives." Also, the number of Americans who said they are "deeply involved in the search for community" increased from 32 percent to 47 percent from 1973 to 1980.[26] Whether or not we agree that there is a sweeping cultural revolution under way, the sentiments of such a social ethic seem to strike a more resonant chord in a growing number of people.

So after an historical and cross-cultural journey the final message of this book is what doubtless will be considered conservative and old-fashioned. Even this may be in the spirit of the times, wherein *Roots* became an overnight sensation and where many Americans seem politically to want to turn back. But I am not advocating a return. We cannot go back to an earlier period in history. What we must do is make a greater effort to shore up the elements of community in the face of advanced urban and industrial conditions.

Nor can we leap suddenly ahead into a new and different era. Some suggest that mass communications eventually will permit the complete demise of the local community in favor of the national and global "village." But overlooked in this view is the paramount necessity in everyday life, if human societies are to persevere, of meaningful, face-to-face contact among people. Most of us realize how important this is in our private lives, and we build our private worlds accordingly. What we are much less aware of is how important it is in our public lives, and that as a social reality such contact is quietly slipping away.

## Notes

1. Larry Long and Diana De Are, *Migration to Non-Metropolitan Areas: Appraising the Trend and Reasons for Moving* (Washington, DC: Bureau of the Census, 1980).
2. Marion Clawson and Peter Hall, *Planning and Urban Growth: An Anglo-American Comparison* (Baltimore: John Hopkins University Press, 1973), p. 215.
3. Cited in Earl Finkler, *Nongrowth as a Planning Alternative: A Preliminary Examination of an Emerging Issue* (Washington, DC: American Society of Planning Officials, 1972).
4. Angus Campbell, *The Sense of Well-Being in America* (New York: McGraw-Hill, 1981), p. 150.
5. Ibid., p. 154.
6. Ibid., p. 152.
7. See Richard P. Appelbaum, *Size, Growth and U.S. Cities* (New York: Praeger, 1978), ch. 6.
8. Ibid., p.101.
9. David Popenoe, "Urban Scale and the Quality of Community Life: A Swedish Community Comparison," *Sociological Inquiry* 53 (Fall 1983): 404-18.
10. For classic statements, see Ralph Borsodi, *Flight from the City* (New York: Harper & Brothers, 1933); and Arthur E. Morgan, *The Community of the Future* (Yellow Springs, OH: Community Service, 1957). A recent statement is Murray Bookchin, *The Limits of the City* (New York: Harper & Row, 1973).
11. See James A. Clapp, *New Towns and Urban Policy* (New York: Dunellen, 1971); and Gurney Breckenfeld, *Columbia and the New Cities* (New York: Ives Washburn, 1971).
12. See Clawson and Hall, *Planning and Urban Growth*; and Frank Schaffer, *The New Town Story* (London: Paladin, 1972).
13. See on communes Rosabeth Moss Kanter, *Community and Commitment* (Cambridge: Harvard University Press, 1972); Benjamin Zablocki, *Alienation and Charisma* (New York: Free Press, 1980); Hugh Gardner, *The Children of Prosperity* (New York: St. Martin's Press, 1978); and Ron E. Roberts, *The New Communes* (Englewood Cliffs, NJ: Prentice-Hall, 1971).
14. Lionel Tiger and Joseph Shepher, *Women in the Kibbutz* (New York: Harcourt Brace Jovanovich, 1975).

15. Jack D. Kasarda and M. Janowitz, "Community Attachment in Mass Society," *American Sociological Review* 39 (June 1974).
16. For a popularized discussion of this problem, see Vance Packard, *A Nation of Strangers* (New York: McKay, 1972).
17. A classic statement of this is Arthur J. Vidich and J. D. Bensman, *Small Town in Mass Society* (Princeton: Princeton University Press, 1968). See also the discussion of vertical and horizontal ties in Roland L. Warren, *The Community in America* (Chicago: Rand McNally, 1972).
18. The best recent statement of this issue is Peter L. Berger and R. J. Neuhaus, *To Empower the People: The Role of Mediating Structures in Public Policy* (Washington, DC: American Enterprise Institute, 1977).
19. Emile Durkheim, *The Division of Labor in Society* (Glencoe, Ill.: Free Press, 1933).
20. See Kevin Lynch, *The Image of the City* (Cambridge: MIT Press, 1969).
21. See David Popenoe, "Urban Sprawl: Some Neglected Sociological Considerations," *Sociology and Social Research* 63 (January 1979).
22. Morris Janowitz, *The Community Press in an Urban Setting* (Chicago: University of Chicago Press, 1952).
23. A similar point of view can be found in Oscar Newman, *Community of Interest* (Garden City, NY: Doubleday/Anchor, 1980).
24. The classic statement is Clarence Perry, *The Neighborhood Unit—Regional Survey of New York and Its Environs* (New York: Regional Plan Association, 1929).
25. "Now, Psychological Man," *New York Times*, October 31, 1980, p. A27.
26. Daniel Yankelovich, *New Rules: Searching for Self-Fulfillment in a World Turned Upside Down* (New York: Random House, 1981).

# Index

Adams, Henry, 14
Allardt, Eric, 133-34
Antiurbanism, 31
Arendt, Hannah, 111, 127
Aristocracy, English, 58
Automobiles, 43-44, 45, 46-47, 55, 120-21. *See also* Transportation
Awkwright, Thomas, 15

Baltimore (Md.), 31
Belgium, 108n32
Belonging. *See* Personal well-being
Berger, Peter, 116
Birmingham (England), metropolitan setting of, 50-54
Birth rates, 79, 128, 144
Boston (Mass.), 31

California, shopping in, 114-15
Campbell, Angus, 133, 145, 155
Canada, 91n13
Capitalism, 55, 112
Career. *See* Life styles
Census, U.S. Bureau of the, 127
Central city. *See* Downtown areas
Change, social, 18-20, 143-57
Chicago (Ill.), 37n4
Churchill, Winston, 41
Cities: decline of, 143-45; economic derivation of, 33-34; growth of, 26, 31-32; physical form of, 18, 32, 34, 49-50, 55-56. *See also* Metropolitan community structure; Urban development
*City, The* (Weber), 4
Class, social. *See* Segregation; Social structure
Clawson, Marion, 64
Clustering. *See* Segregation

Coalbrookdale (England), 15
Coleman, James, 96
Collectivism, 121, 123-27
Communalism, 29-30, 147-48
Communities, functioning of. *See* Collectivism
Community life: changes in, 18-20, 143-57; medieval English, 14-16, 54, 57. *See also* Life styles; Metropolitan community structure
Community structure. *See* Metropolitan community structure
Comparative analysis, 3-7, 55-72. *See also* Metropolitan community structure
Consumership, 45, 82, 89-90
Cottage industries, 15, 35
Creativity, 122-23
Crime, 124-25, 126, 137. *See also* Life styles
Cromford (England), 15
Cultural attachment, 137-39, 151-52

Dalarna (Sweden), 27
Darby, Alexander, 15, 16
Decentralization, 143-48
Demetropolitanization, 143-45
Demography, urban, 7-8. *See also* name of city or nation
Denmark, 108n32
Dickens, Charles, 16
Dormitory areas, 35-36
Downtown areas, 48-49, 52, 66-68, 120
Durkheim, Emile, 151

Egalitarianism, Sweden and, 27
Elderly, 129
Emerson, Ralph Waldo, 30-31
Enclosure movement, 17, 27